MARY STUART

by

Alexandre Dumas

Copyright © 2012 Read Books Ltd.
This book is copyright and may not be
reproduced or copied in any way without
the express permission of the publisher in writing

British Library Cataloguing-in-Publication Data
A catalogue record for this book is available from the
British Library

Contents

Alexandre Dumas 5
CHAPTER I 7
CHAPTER II. 28
CHAPTER III. 48
CHAPTER IV 79
CHAPTER V. 87
CHAPTER VI 144
CHAPTER VII 161
CHAPTER VIII 195
CHAPTER IX 228
CHAPTER X. 266

Alexandre Dumas

Alexandre Dumas was born in Villers-Cotterêts, France in 1802. His parents were poor, but their heritage and good reputation – Alexandre's father had been a general in Napoleon's army – provided Alexandre with opportunities for good employment. In 1822, Dumas moved to Paris to work for future king Louis Philippe I in the Palais Royal. It was here that he began to write for magazines and the theatre.

In 1829 and 1830 respectively, Dumas produced the plays Henry III and His Court and Christine, both of which met with critical acclaim and financial success. As a result, he was able to commit himself full-time to writing. Despite the turbulent economic times which followed the Revolution of 1830, Dumas turned out to have something of an entrepreneurial streak, and did well for himself in this decade. He founded a production studio that turned out hundreds of stories under his creative direction, and began to produce serialised novels for newspapers which were widely read by the French public. It was over the next two decades, as a now famous and much loved author of romantic and adventuring sagas, that Dumas produced his best-known works – the D'Artagnan romances, including The Three Musketeers, in 1844, and The Count of Monte Cristo, in 1846.

Dumas made a lot of money from his writing, but he was almost constantly penniless as a result of his extravagant lifestyle and love of women. In 1851 he fled his creditors to Belgium, and then Russia, and then Italy, not returning to Paris until 1864. Dumas died in Puys, France, in 1870, at the age of 68. He is now enshrined in the Panthéon of Paris alongside fellow authors Victor Hugo and Emile Zola. Since his death, his fiction has been translated into almost a hundred languages, and has formed the basis for more than 200 motion pictures.

CHAPTER I

Some royal names are predestined to misfortune: in France, there is the name "Henry". Henry I was poisoned, Henry II was killed in a tournament, Henry III and Henry IV were assassinated. As to Henry V, for whom the past is so fatal already, God alone knows what the future has in store for him.

In Scotland, the unlucky name is "Stuart". Robert I, founder of the race, died at twenty-eight of a lingering illness. Robert II, the most fortunate of the family, was obliged to pass a part of his life, not merely in retirement, but also in the dark, on account of inflammation of the eyes, which made them blood-red. Robert III succumbed to grief, the death of one son and the captivity of other. James I was stabbed by Graham in the abbey of the Black Monks of Perth. James II was killed at the siege of Roxburgh, by a splinter from a burst cannon. James III was assassinated by an unknown hand in a mill, where he had taken refuge during the battle of Sauchie. James IV, wounded by two arrows and a blow from a halberd, fell amidst his nobles on the battlefield of Flodden. James V died of grief at the loss of his two sons, and of remorse for the execution of Hamilton. James VI, destined to unite on his head the two crowns of Scotland and England, son of a father who had been assassinated, led a melancholy and timorous existence, between the scaffold of his mother, Mary Stuart, and that of his son, Charles I. Charles II spent a portion of his life in exile. James II died in it. The Chevalier Saint-George, after having been proclaimed King of Scotland as James VIII, and of England and Ireland as James III, was forced to flee, without having been able to give his arms even the lustre of a defeat. His son, Charles Edward, after the skirmish at Derby and the battle of Culloden, hunted from mountain to mountain, pursued from rock to rock, swimming from shore to shore, picked up half naked by a French vessel, betook himself to Florence to die there, without the European courts having ever consented to recognise him as a sovereign. Finally, his brother, Henry Benedict, the last heir of the Stuarts, having lived on a pension of three thousand pounds sterling, granted him by George III, died completely forgotten, bequeathing to the House of Hanover all the crown jewels which James II had carried off when he passed over to the Continent in 1688—a tardy but complete recognition of the legitimacy of the family which had succeeded his.

In the midst of this unlucky race, Mary Stuart was the favourite of misfortune. As Brantome has said of her, "Whoever desires to write about this illustrious queen of Scotland has, in her, two very, large subjects, the one her life, the other her death," Brantome had known her on one of the most mournful occasions of her life—at the moment when she was quitting France for Scotland.

It was on the 9th of August, 1561, after having lost her mother and her husband in the same year, that Mary Stuart, Dowager of France and Queen of Scotland at nineteen, escorted by her uncles, Cardinals Guise and Lorraine, by the Duke and Duchess of Guise, by the Duc d'Aumale and M. de Nemours, arrived at Calais, where two galleys were waiting to take her to Scotland, one commanded by M. de Mevillon and the other by Captain Albize. She remained six days in the town. At last, on the 15th of the month, after the saddest adieus to her family, accompanied by Messieurs d'Aumale, d'Elboeuf, and Damville, with many nobles, among whom were Brantome and Chatelard, she embarked in M. Mevillon's galley, which was immediately ordered to put out to sea, which it did with the aid of oars, there not being sufficient wind to make use of the sails.

Mary Stuart was then in the full bloom of her beauty, beauty even more brilliant in its mourning garb—a beauty so wonderful that it shed around her a charm which no one whom she wished to please could escape, and which was fatal to almost everyone. About this time, too, someone made her the subject of a song, which, as even her rivals confessed, contained no more than the truth. It was, so it was said, by M. de Maison-Fleur, a cavalier equally accomplished in arms and letters: Here it is:—

"In robes of whiteness, lo, Full sad and mournfully, Went pacing to and fro Beauty's divinity; A shaft in hand she bore From Cupid's cruel store, And he, who fluttered round, Bore, o'er his blindfold eyes And o'er his head uncrowned, A veil of mournful guise, Whereon the words were wrought: 'You perish or are caught.'"

Yes, at this moment, Mary Stuart, in her deep mourning of white, was more lovely than ever; for great tears were trickling down her cheeks, as, weaving a handkerchief, standing on the quarterdeck, she who was so grieved to set out, bowed farewell to those who were so grieved to remain.

At last, in half an hour's time, the harbour was left behind; the vessel was out at sea. Suddenly, Mary heard loud cries behind her: a boat coming in under press of sail, through her pilot's ignorance had struck upon a rock in such a manner that it was split open, and after having trembled and groaned for a moment like someone wounded, began to be swallowed up, amid the terrified screams of all the crew. Mary, horror-stricken, pale, dumb, and motionless, watched her gradually sink, while her unfortunate crew, as the keel disappeared, climbed into the yards and shrouds, to delay their death-agony a few minutes; finally, keel, yards, masts, all were engulfed in the ocean's gaping jaws. For a moment there remained some black specks, which in turn disappeared one after another; then wave followed upon wave, and the spectators of this horrible tragedy, seeing the sea calm and solitary as if nothing had happened, asked themselves if it was not a vision that had appeared to them and vanished.

"Alas!" cried Mary, falling on a seat and leaning both arms an the vessel's stern, "what a sad omen for such a sad voyage!" Then, once more fixing on the receding harbour her eyes, dried for a moment by terror, and beginning to moisten anew, "Adieu, France!" she murmured, "adieu, France!" and for five hours she remained thus, weeping and murmuring, "Adieu, France! adieu, France!"

Darkness fell while she was still lamenting; and then, as

the view was blotted out and she was summoned to supper, "It is indeed now, dear France," said she, rising, "that I really lose you, since jealous night heaps mourning upon mourning, casting a black veil before my sight. Adieu then, one last time, dear France; for never shall I see you more."

With these words, she went below, saying that she was the very opposite of Dido, who, after the departure of AEneas, had done nothing but look at the waves, while she, Mary, could not take her eyes off the land. Then everyone gathered round her to try to divert and console her. But she, growing sadder, and not being able to respond, so overcome was she with tears, could hardly eat; and, having had a bed got ready on the stern deck, she sent for the steersman, and ordered him if he still saw land at daybreak, to come and wake her immediately. On this point Mary was favoured; for the wind having dropped, when daybreak came the vessel was still within sight of France.

It was a great joy when, awakened by the steersman, who had not forgotten the order he had received, Mary raised herself on her couch, and through the window that she had had opened, saw once more the beloved shore. But at five o'clock in the morning, the wind having freshened, the vessel rapidly drew farther away, so that soon the land completely disappeared. Then Mary fell back upon her bed, pale as death, murmuring yet once again—"Adieu, France! I shall see thee no more."

Indeed, the happiest years of her life had just passed away in this France that she so much regretted. Born amid the first religious troubles, near the bedside of her dying father, the cradle mourning was to stretch for her to the grave, and her stay in France had been a ray of sunshine in her night. Slandered from her birth, the report was so generally spread abroad that she was malformed, and that she could not live to grow up, that one day her mother, Mary of Guise, tired of these false rumours, undressed her and showed her naked to the English ambassador, who had come, on the part of Henry VIII, to ask her in marriage for the Prince of Wales, himself only five years old. Crowned at nine months by Cardinal Beaton, archbishop of St. Andrews, she was immediately hidden by her mother, who was afraid of treacherous dealing in the King of England, in Stirling Castle. Two years later, not finding even this fortress safe enough, she removed her to an island in the middle of the Lake of Menteith, where a priory, the only building in the place, provided an asylum for the royal child and for four young girls born in the same year as herself, having like her the sweet name which is an anagram of the word "aimer," and who, quitting her neither in her good nor in her evil fortune, were called the "Queen's Marys". They were Mary Livingston, Mary Fleming, Mary Seyton, and Mary Beaton. Mary stayed in this priory till Parliament, having approved her marriage with the French dauphin, son of Henry II, she was taken to Dumbarton Castle, to await the moment of departure. There she was entrusted to M. de Breze, sent by Henry II to-fetch her. Having set out in the French galleys anchored at the mouth of the Clyde, Mary, after having been hotly pursued by the

English fleet, entered Brest harbour, 15th August, 1548, one year after the death of Francis! Besides the queen's four Marys, the vessels also brought to France three of her natural brothers, among whom was the Prior of St. Andrews, James Stuart, who was later to abjure the Catholic faith, and with the title of Regent, and under the name of the Earl of Murray, to become so fatal to poor Mary. From Brest, Mary went to St. Germain-en-Laye, where Henry II, who had just ascended the throne, overwhelmed her with caresses, and then sent her to a convent where the heiresses of the noblest French houses were brought up. There Mary's happy qualities developed. Born with a woman's heart and a man's head, Mary not only acquired all the accomplishments which constituted the education of a future queen, but also that real knowledge which is the object of the truly learned.

Thus, at fourteen, in the Louvre, before Henry II, Catherine de Medici, and the whole court, she delivered a discourse in Latin of her own composition, in which she maintained that it becomes women to cultivate letters, and that it is unjust and tyrannical to deprive flowery of their perfumes, by banishing young girls from all but domestic cares. One can imagine in what manner a future queen, sustaining such a thesis, was likely to be welcomed in the most lettered and pedantic court in Europe. Between the literature of Rabelais and Marot verging on their decline, and that of Ronsard and Montaigne reaching their zenith, Mary became a queen of poetry, only too happy never to have to wear another crown than that which Ronsard,

Dubellay, Maison-Fleur, and Brantome placed daily on her head. But she was predestined. In the midst of those fetes which a waning chivalry was trying to revive came the fatal joust of Tournelles: Henry II, struck by a splinter of a lance for want of a visor, slept before his time with his ancestors, and Mary Stuart ascended the throne of France, where, from mourning for Henry, she passed to that for her mother, and from mourning for her mother to that for her husband. Mary felt this last loss both as woman and as poet; her heart burst forth into bitter tears and plaintive harmonies. Here are some lines that she composed at this time:—

"Into my song of woe, Sung to a low sad air, My cruel grief I throw, For loss beyond compare; In bitter sighs and tears Go by my fairest years.

Was ever grief like mine Imposed by destiny? Did ever lady pine, In high estate, like me, Of whom both heart and eye Within the coffin lie?

Who, in the tender spring And blossom of my youth, Taste all the sorrowing Of life's extremest ruth, And take delight in nought Save in regretful thought.

All that was sweet and gay Is now a pain to see; The sunniness of day Is black as night to me; All that was my delight Is hidden from my sight.

My heart and eye, indeed, One face, one image know, The which this mournful weed On my sad face doth show, Dyed with the violet's tone That is the lover's own.

Tormented by my ill, I go from place to place, But wander as I will My woes can nought efface; My most of bad and good I find in solitude.

But wheresoe'er I stay, In meadow or in copse, Whether at break of day Or when the twilight drops, My heart goes sighing on, Desiring one that's gone.

If sometimes to the skies My weary gaze I lift, His gently shining eyes Look from the cloudy drift, Or stooping o'er the wave I see him in the grave.

Or when my bed I seek, And-sleep begins to steal, Again I hear him speak, Again his touch I feel; In work or leisure, he Is ever near to me.

No other thing I see, However fair displayed, By which my heart will be A tributary made, Not having the perfection Of that, my lost affection.

Here make an end, my verse, Of this thy sad lament, Whose burden shall rehearse Pure love of true intent, Which separation's stress Will never render less."

"It was then," says Brantorne, "that it was delightful to see her; for the whiteness of her countenance and of her veil contended together; but finally the artificial white yielded, and the snow-like pallor of her face vanquished the other. For it was thus," he adds, "that from the moment she became a widow, I always saw her with her pale hue, as long as I had the honour of seeing her in France, and Scotland, where she had to go in eighteen months' time, to her very great regret, after her widowhood, to pacify her kingdom, greatly divided by religious troubles. Alas! she had neither the wish nor the will for it, and I have often heard her say so, with a fear of this journey like death; for she preferred a hundred times to dwell in France as a dowager queen, and to content herself with Touraine and Poitou for her jointure, than to go and reign over there in her wild country; but her uncles, at least some of them, not all, advised her, and even urged her to it, and deeply repented their error."

Mary was obedient, as we have seen, and she began her journey under such auspices that when she lost sight of land she was like to die. Then it was that the poetry of her soul found expression in these famous lines:

"Farewell, delightful land of France,
My motherland,
The best beloved!
Foster-nurse of my young years!
Farewell, France, and farewell my happy days!
The ship that separates our loves
Has borne away but half of me;
One part is left thee and is throe,
And I confide it to thy tenderness,
That thou may'st hold in mind the other part.'"

[Translator's note.-It has not been found possible to make a rhymed version of these lines without sacrificing the simplicity which is their chief charm.]

This part of herself that Mary left in France was the body of the young king, who had taken with him all poor Mary's happiness into his tomb.

Mary had but one hope remaining, that the sight of the English fleet would compel her little squadron to turn back; but she had to fulfil her destiny. This same day, a fog, a very unusual occurrence in summer-time, extended all over the Channel, and caused her to escape the fleet; for it was such a dense fog that one could not see from stern to mast. It lasted the whole of Sunday, the day after the departure, and did not lift till the following day, Monday, at eight o'clock in the morning. The little flotilla, which all this time had been sailing haphazard, had got among so many reefs that if the fog had lasted some minutes longer the galley would certainly have grounded on some rock, and would have perished like the vessel that had been seen engulfed on leaving port. But, thanks to the fog's clearing, the pilot recognised the Scottish coast, and, steering his four boats with great skill through all the dangers, on the 20th August he put in at Leith, where no preparation had been made for the queen's reception. Nevertheless, scarcely had she arrived there than the chief persons of the town met together and came to felicitate her. Meanwhile, they hastily collected some wretched nags, with harness all falling in pieces, to conduct the queen to Edinburgh.

At sight of this, Mary could not help weeping again; for she thought of the splendid palfreys and hackneys of her French knights and ladies, and at this first view Scotland appeared to-her in all its poverty. Next day it was to appear to her in all its wildness.

After having passed one night at Holyrood Palace, "during which," says Brantome, "five to six hundred rascals from the town, instead of letting her sleep, came to give her a wild morning greeting on wretched fiddles and little rebecks," she expressed a wish to hear mass. Unfortunately, the people of Edinburgh belonged almost entirely to the Reformed religion; so that, furious at the queen's giving such a proof of papistry at her first appearance, they entered the church by force, armed with knives, sticks and stones, with the intention of putting to death the poor priest, her chaplain. He left the altar, and took refuge near the queen, while Mary's brother, the Prior of St. Andrews, who was more inclined from this time forward to be a soldier than an ecclesiastic, seized a sword, and, placing himself between the people and the queen, declared that he would kill with his own hand the first man who should take another step. This firmness, combined with the queen's imposing and dignified air, checked the zeal of the Reformers.

As we have said, Mary had arrived in the midst of all the heat of the first religious wars. A zealous Catholic, like all her family on the maternal side, she inspired the Huguenots with the gravest fears: besides, a rumour had got about that Mary, instead of landing at Leith, as she had been obliged by the fog, was to land at Aberdeen. There, it was said, she would have found the Earl of Huntly, one of the peers who had remained loyal to the Catholic faith, and who, next to the family of Hamilton, was, the nearest and most powerful ally of the royal house. Seconded by him and by twenty thousand soldiers from the north, she would then have marched upon Edinburgh, and have re-established the Catholic faith throughout Scotland. Events were not slow to prove that this accusation was false.

As we have stated, Mary was much attached to the Prior of St. Andrews, a son of James V and of a noble descendant of the Earls of Mar, who had been very handsome in her youth, and who, in spite of the well-known love for her of James V, and the child who had resulted, had none the less wedded Lord Douglas of Lochleven, by whom she had had two other sons, the elder named William and the younger George, who were thus half-brothers of the regent. Now, scarcely had she reascended the throne than Mary had restored to the Prior of St. Andrews the title of Earl of Mar, that of his maternal ancestors, and as that of the Earl of Murray had lapsed since the death of the famous Thomas Randolph, Mary, in her sisterly friendship for James Stuart, hastened to add, this title to those which she had already bestowed upon him.

But here difficulties and complications arose; for the new Earl of Murray, with his character, was not a man to content himself with a barren title, while the estates which were crown property since the extinction of the male branch of the old earls, had been gradually encroached upon by powerful neighbours, among whom was the famous Earl of Huntly, whom we have already mentioned: the result was that, as the queen judged that in this quarter her orders would probably encounter opposition, under pretext of visiting her possessions in the north, she placed herself at the head of a small army, commanded by her brother, the Earl of Mar and Murray.

The Earl of Huntly was the less duped by the apparent pretext of this expedition, in that his son, John Cordon, for some abuse of his powers, had just been condemned to a temporary imprisonment. He, notwithstanding, made every possible submission to the queen, sending messengers in advance to invite-her to rest in his castle; and following up the messengers in person, to renew his invitation viva voce. Unfortunately, at the very moment when he was about to join the queen, the governor of Inverness, who was entirely devoted to him, was refusing to allow Mary to enter this castle, which was a royal one. It is true that Murray, aware that it does not do to hesitate in the face of such rebellions, had already had him executed for high treason.

This new act of firmness showed Huntly that the young queen was not disposed to allow the Scottish lords a resumption of the almost sovereign power humbled by her father; so that, in spite of the extremely kind reception she accorded him, as he learned while in camp that his son, having escaped from prison, had just put himself at the head of his vassals, he was afraid that he should be thought, as doubtless he was, a party to the rising, and he set out the same night to assume command of his troops, his mind made up, as Mary only had with her seven to eight thousand men, to risk a battle, giving out, however, as Buccleuch had done in his attempt to snatch James V from the hands of the Douglases, that it was not at the queen he was aiming, but solely at the regent, who kept her under his tutelage and perverted her good intentions.

Murray, who knew that often the entire peace of a reign depends on the firmness one displays at its beginning, immediately summoned all the northern barons whose estates bordered on his, to march against Huntly. All obeyed, for the house of Cordon was already so powerful that each feared it might become still more so; but, however, it was clear that if there was hatred for the subject there was no great affection for the queen, and that the greater number came without fixed intentions and with the idea of being led by circumstances.

The two armies encountered near Aberdeen. Murray at once posted the troops he had brought from Edinburgh, and of which he was sure, on the top of rising ground, and drew up in tiers on the hill slope all his northern allies. Huntly advanced resolutely upon them, and attacked his neighbours the Highlanders, who after a short resistance retired in disorder. His men immediately threw away their lances, and, drawing their swords, crying, "Cordon, Cordon!" pursued the fugitives, and believed they had already gained the battle, when they suddenly ran right against the main body of Murray's army, which remained motionless as a rampart of iron, and which, with its long lances, had the advantage of its adversaries, who were armed only with their claymores. It was then the turn of the Cordons to draw back, seeing which, the northern clans rallied and returned to the fight, each soldier having a sprig of heather in his cap that his comrades might recognise him. This unexpected movement determined the day: the Highlanders ran down the hillside like a torrent, dragging along with them everyone who could have wished to oppose their passage. Then Murray seeing that the moment had come for changing the defeat into a rout, charged with his entire cavalry: Huntly, who was very stout and very heavily armed, fell and was crushed beneath the horses' feet; John Cordon, taken prisoner in his flight, was executed at Aberdeen three days afterwards; finally, his brother, too young to undergo the same fate at this time, was shut up in a dungeon and executed later, the day he reached the age of sixteen.

Mary had been present at the battle, and the calm and courage she displayed had made a lively impression on her wild defenders, who all along the road had heard her say that she would have liked to be a man, to pass her days on horseback, her nights under a tent, to wear a coat of mail, a helmet, a buckler, and at her side a broadsword.

Mary made her entry into Edinburgh amid general enthusiasm; for this expedition against the Earl of Huntly, who was a Catholic, had been very popular among the inhabitants, who had no very clear idea of the real motives which had caused her to undertake it: They were of the Reformed faith, the earl was a papist, there was an enemy the less; that is all they thought about. Now, therefore; the Scotch, amid their acclamations, whether viva voce or by written demands, expressed the wish that their queen, who was without issue by Francis II, should re-marry: Mary agreed to this, and, yielding to the prudent advice of those about her, she decided to consult upon this marriage Elizabeth, whose heir she was, in her title of granddaughter of Henry VII, in the event of the Queen of England's dying without posterity. Unfortunately, she had not always acted with like circumspection; for at the death of Mary Tudor, known as Bloody Mary, she had laid claim to the throne of Henry VIII, and, relying on the illegitimacy of Elizabeth's birth, had with the dauphin assumed sovereignty over Scotland, England, and Ireland, and had had coins struck with this new title, and plate engraved with these new armorial bearings.

Elizabeth was nine years older than Mary—that is to say, that at this time she had not yet attained her thirtieth year; she was not merely her rival as queen, then, but as woman. As regards education, she could sustain comparison with advantage; for if she had less charm of mind, she had more solidity of judgment: versed in politics, philosophy, history; rhetoric, poetry and music, besides English, her maternal tongue, she spoke and wrote to perfection Greek, Latin, French, Italian and Spanish; but while Elizabeth excelled Mary on this point, in her turn Mary was more beautiful, and above all more attractive, than her rival. Elizabeth had, it is true, a majestic and agreeable appearance, bright quick eyes, a dazzlingly white complexion; but she had red hair, a large foot,—[Elizabeth bestowed a pair of her shoes on the University of Oxford; their size would point to their being those of a man of average stature.]—and a powerful hand, while Mary, on the contrary, with her beautiful ashy-fair hair,—[Several historians assert that Mary Stuart had black hair; but Brantome, who had seen it, since, as we have said, he accompanied her to Scotland, affirms that it was fair. And, so saying, he (the executioner) took off her headdress, in a contemptuous manner, to display her hair already white, that while alive, however, she feared not to show, nor yet to twist and frizz as in the days when it was so beautiful and so fair.]—her noble open forehead, eyebrows which could be only blamed for being so regularly arched that they looked as if drawn by a pencil, eyes continually beaming with the witchery of fire, a nose of perfect Grecian outline, a mouth so ruby red and gracious that it seemed that, as a flower opens but to let its perfume escape, so it could not open but to give passage to gentle words, with a neck white and graceful as a swan's, hands of alabaster, with a form like a goddess's and a foot like a child's, Mary was a harmony in which the most ardent enthusiast for sculptured form could have found nothing to reproach.

This was indeed Mary's great and real crime: one single imperfection in face or figure, and she would not have died upon the scaffold. Besides, to Elizabeth, who had never seen her, and who consequently could only judge by hearsay, this beauty was a great cause of uneasiness and of jealousy, which she could not even disguise, and which showed itself unceasingly in eager questions. One day when she was chatting with James Melville about his mission to her court, Mary's offer to be guided by Elizabeth in her choice of a husband,—a choice which the queen of England had seemed at first to wish to see fixed on the Earl of Leicester,—she led the Scotch ambassador into a cabinet, where she showed him several portraits with labels in her own handwriting: the first was one of the Earl of Leicester. As this nobleman was precisely the suitor chosen by Elizabeth, Melville asked the queen to give it him to show to his mistress; but Elizabeth refused, saying that it was the only one she had. Melville then replied, smiling, that being in possession of the original she might well part with the copy; but Elizabeth would on no account consent. This little discussion ended, she showed him the portrait of Mary Stuart, which she kissed very tenderly, expressing to Melville a great wish to see his mistress. "That is very easy, madam," he replied: "keep your room, on the pretext that you are indisposed, and set out incognito for Scotland, as King James V set out for France when he wanted to see Madeleine de Valois, whom he afterwards married."

"Alas!" replied Elizabeth, "I would like to do so, but it is not so easy as you think. Nevertheless, tell your queen that I love her tenderly, and that I wish we could live more in friendship than we have done up to the present". Then passing to a subject which she seemed to have wanted to broach for a long time, "Melville," she continued, "tell me frankly, is my sister as beautiful as they say?"

"She has that reputation," replied Melville; "but I cannot give your Majesty any idea of hex beauty, having no point of comparison."

"I will give you one," the queen said. "Is she more beautiful than I?"

"Madam," replied Melville, "you are the most beautiful woman in England, and Mary Stuart is the most beautiful woman in Scotland."

"Then which of the two is the taller?" asked Elizabeth,

who was not entirely satisfied by this answer, clever as it was.

"My mistress, madam," responded Melville; "I am obliged to confess it."

"Then she is too tall," Elizabeth said sharply, "for I am tall enough. And what are her favourite amusements?" she continued.

"Madam," Melville replied, "hunting, riding, performing on the lute and the harpischord."

"Is she skilled upon the latter?" Elizabeth inquired. "Oh yes, madam," answered Melville; "skilled enough for a queen."

There the conversation stopped; but as Elizabeth was herself an excellent musician, she commanded Lord Hunsdon to bring Melville to her at a time when she was at her harpischord, so that he could hear her without her seeming to have the air of playing for him. In fact, the same day, Hunsdon, agreeably to her instructions, led the ambassador into a gallery separated from the queen's apartment merely by tapestry, so that his guide having raised it. Melville at his leisure could hear Elizabeth, who did not turn round until she had finished the piece, which, however, she was playing with much skill. When she saw Melville, she pretended to fly into a passion, and even wanted to strike him; but her anger calmed down by little and little at the ambassador's compliments, and ceased altogether when he admitted that Mary Stuart was not her equal. But this was not all: proud of her triumph, Elizabeth desired also that Melville should see her dance. Accordingly, she kept back her despatches for two days that he might be present at a ball that she was giving. These despatches, as we have said, contained the wish that Mary Stuart should espouse Leicester; but this proposal could not be taken seriously. Leicester, whose personal worth was besides sufficiently mediocre, was of birth too inferior to aspire to the hand of the daughter of so many kings; thus Mary replied that such an alliance would not become her. Meanwhile, something strange and tragic came to pass.

CHAPTER II

Among the lords who had followed Mary Stuart to Scotland was, as we have mentioned, a young nobleman named Chatelard, a true type of the nobility of that time, a nephew of Bayard on his mother's side, a poet and a knight, talented and courageous, and attached to Marshal Damville, of whose household he formed one. Thanks to this high position, Chatelard, throughout her stay in France, paid court to Mary Stuart, who, in the homage he rendered her in verse, saw nothing more than those poetical declarations of gallantry customary in that age, and with which she especially was daily overwhelmed. But it happened that about the time when Chatelard was most in love with the queen she was obliged to leave France, as we have said. Then Marshal Damville, who knew nothing of Chatelard's passion, and who himself, encouraged by Mary's kindness, was among the candidates to succeed Francis II as husband, set out for Scotland with the poor exile, taking Chatelard with him, and, not imagining he would find a rival in him, he made a confidant of him, and left him with Mary when he was obliged to leave her, charging the young poet to support with her the interests of his suit. This post as confidant brought Mary and Chatelard more together; and, as in her capacity as poet, the queen treated him like a brother, he made bold in his passion to risk all to obtain another title. Accordingly, one evening he got into Mary Stuart's room, and hid himself under the bed; but at the moment when the queen was beginning to undress, a little dog she had began to yelp so loudly that her women came running at his barking, and, led by this indication, perceived Chatelard. A woman easily pardons a crime for which too great love is the excuse: Mary Stuart was woman before being queen—she pardoned.

But this kindness only increased Chatelard's confidence: he put down the reprimand he had received to the presence of the queen's women, and supposed that if she had been alone she would have forgiven him still more completely; so that, three weeks after, this same scene was repeated. But this time, Chatelard, discovered in a cupboard, when the queen was already in bed, was placed under arrest.

The moment was badly chosen: such a scandal, just when the queen was about to re-marry, was fatal to Mary, let alone to Chatelard. Murray took the affair in hand, and, thinking that a public trial could alone save his sister's reputation, he urged the prosecution with such vigour, that Chatelard, convicted of the crime of lese-majeste, was condemned to death. Mary entreated her brother that Chatelard might be sent back to France; but Murray made her see what terrible consequences such a use of her right of pardon might have, so that Mary was obliged to let justice take its course: Chatelard was led to execution. Arrived on the scaffold, which was set up before the queen's palace, Chatelard, who had declined the services of a priest, had Ronsard's Ode on Death read; and when the reading, which he followed with evident pleasure, was ended, he turned—towards the queen's windows, and, having cried out for the last time, "Adieu, loveliest and most cruel of princesses!" he stretched out his neck to the executioner, without displaying any repentance or uttering any complaint. This death made all the more impression upon Mary, that she did not dare to show her sympathy openly.

Meanwhile there was a rumour that the queen of Scotland was consenting to a new marriage, and several suitors came forward, sprung from the principal reigning families of Europe: first, the Archduke Charles, third son of the Emperor of Germany; then the Duke of Anjou, who afterwards became Henry III. But to wed a foreign prince was to give up her claims to the English crown. So Mary refused, and, making a merit of this to Elizabeth, she cast her eyes on a relation of the latter's, Henry Stuart, Lord Darnley, son of the Earl of Lennox. Elizabeth, who had nothing plausible to urge against this marriage, since the Queen of Scotland not only chose an Englishman for husband, but was marrying into her own family, allowed the Earl of Lennox and his son to go to the Scotch court, reserving it to herself, if matters appeared to take a serious turn, to recall them both—a command which they would be constrained to obey, since all their property was in England.

Darnley was eighteen years of age: he was handsome, well-made, elegant; he talked in that attractive manner of the young nobles of the French and English courts that Mary no longer heard since her exile in Scotland; she let herself be deceived by these appearances, and did not see that under this brilliant exterior Darnley hid utter insignificance, dubious courage, and a fickle and churlish character. It is true that he came to her under the auspices of a man whose influence was as striking as the risen fortune which gave him the opportunity to exert it. We refer to David Rizzio.

David Rizzio, who played such a great part in the life of Mary Stuart, whose strange favour for him has given her enemies, probably without any cause, such cruel weapons against her, was the son of a Turin musician burdened with a numerous family, who, recognising in him a pronounced musical taste, had him instructed in the first principles of the art. At the age of fifteen he had left his father's house and had gone on foot to Nice, where the Duke of Savoy held his court; there he entered the service of the Duke of Moreto, and this lord having been appointed, some years afterwards, to the Scottish embassy, Rizzio followed him to Scotland. As this young man had a very fine voice, and accompanied on the viol and fiddle songs of which both the airs and the words were of his own composition, the ambassador spoke of him to Mary, who wished to see him. Rizzio, full of confidence in himself, and seeing in the queen's desire a road to success, hastened to obey her command, sang before her, and pleased her. She begged him then of Moreto, making no more of it than if she had asked of him a thoroughbred dog or a well-trained falcon. Moreta presented him to her, delighted at finding such an opportunity to pay his court; but scarcely was Rizzio in her service than Mary discovered that music was the least of his gifts, that he possessed, besides that, education if not profound at least varied, a supple mind, a lively imagination, gentle ways, and at the same time much boldness and presumption. He reminded her of those Italian artists whom she had seen at the French court, and spoke to her the tongue of Marot and Ronsard, whose most beautiful poems he knew by heart: this was more than enough to please Mary Stuart. In a short time he became her favourite, and meanwhile the place of secretary for the French despatches falling vacant, Rizzio was provided for with it.

Darnley, who wished to succeed at all costs, enlisted Rizzio in his interests, unconscious that he had no need of this support; and as, on her side, Mary, who had fallen in love with him at first sight, fearing some new intrigue of Elizabeth's, hastened on this union so far as the proprieties permitted, the affair moved forward with wonderful rapidity; and in the midst of public rejoicing, with the approbation of the nobility, except for a small minority, with Murray at its head, the marriage was solemnised under the happiest auspices, 29th July 1565. Two days before, Darnley and his father, the Earl of Lennox, had received a command to return to London, and as they had not obeyed it, a week after the celebration of the marriage they learned that the Countess of Lennox, the only one of the family remaining in Elizabeth's power, had been arrested and taken to the Tower. Thus Elizabeth, in spite of her dissimulation, yielding to that first impulse of violence that she always had such trouble to overcome, publicly displayed her resentment.

However, Elizabeth was not the woman to be satisfied with useless vengeance: she soon released the countess, and turned her eyes towards Murray, the most discontented of the nobles in opposition, who by this marriage was losing all his personal influence. It was thus easy for Elizabeth to put arms in his hand. In fact, when he had failed in his first attempt to seize Darnley, he called to his aid the Duke of Chatellerault, Glencairn, Argyll, and Rothes, and collecting what partisans they could, they openly rebelled against the queen. This was the first ostensible act of that hatred which was afterwards so fatal to Mary.

The queen, on her side, appealed to her nobles, who in response hastened to rally to her, so that in a month's time she found herself at the head of the finest army that ever a king of Scotland had raised. Darnley assumed the command of this magnificent assembly, mounted on a superb horse, arrayed in gilded armour; and accompanied by the queen, who, in a riding habit, with pistols at her saddle-bow, wished to make the campaign with him, that she might not quit his side for a moment. Both were young, both were handsome, and they left Edinburgh amidst the cheers of the people and the army.

Murray and his accomplices did not even try to stand against them, and the campaign consisted of such rapid and complex marches and counter-marches, that this rebellion is called the Run-about Raid-that is to say, the run in every sense of the word. Murray and the rebels withdrew into England, where Elizabeth, while seeming to condemn their unlucky attempt, afforded them all the assistance they needed.

Mary returned to Edinburgh delighted at the success

of her two first campaigns, not suspecting that this new good fortune was the last she would have, and that there her short-lived prosperity would cease. Indeed, she soon saw that in Darnley she had given herself not a devoted and very attentive husband, as she had believed, but an imperious and brutal master, who, no longer having any motive for concealment, showed himself to her just as he was, a man of disgraceful vices, of which drunkenness and debauchery was the least. Accordingly, serious differences were not long in springing up in this royal household.

Darnley in wedding Mary had not become king, but merely the queen's husband. To confer on him authority nearly equalling a regent's, it was necessary that Mary should grant him what was termed the crown matrimonial—a crown Francis II had worn during his short royalty, and that Mary, after Darnley's conduct to herself, had not the slightest intention of bestowing on him. Thus, to whatever entreaties he made, in whatever form they were wrapped, Mary merely replied with an unvaried and obstinate refusal. Darnley, amazed at this force of will in a young queen who had loved him enough to raise him to her, and not believing that she could find it in herself, sought in her entourage for some secret and influential adviser who might have inspired her with it. His suspicions fell on Rizzio.

In reality, to whatever cause Rizzio owed his power (and to even the most clear-sighted historians this point has always remained obscure), be it that he ruled as lover, be it that he advised as minister, his counsels as long as he lived were always given for the greater glory of the queen. Sprung from so low, he at least wished to show himself worthy, of having risen so high, and owing everything to Mary, he tried to repay her with devotion. Thus Darnley was not mistaken, and it was indeed Rizzio who, in despair at having helped to bring about a union which he foresaw must become so unfortunate, gave Mary the advice not to give up any of her power to one who already possessed much more than he deserved, in possessing her person.

Darnley, like all persons of both weak and violent character, disbelieved in the persistence of will in others, unless this will was sustained by an outside influence. He thought that in ridding himself of Rizzio he could not fail to gain the day, since, as he believed, he alone was opposing the grant of this great desire of his, the crown matrimonial. Consequently, as Rizzio was disliked by the nobles in proportion as his merits had raised him above them, it was easy for Darnley to organise a conspiracy, and James Douglas of Morton, chancellor of the kingdom, consented to act as chief.

This is the second time since the beginning of our narrative that we inscribe this name Douglas, so often pronounced, in Scottish history, and which at this time, extinct in the elder branch, known as the Black Douglases, was perpetuated in the younger branch, known as the Red Douglases. It was an ancient, noble, and powerful family, which, when the descent in the male line from Robert Bruce had lapsed, disputed the royal title with the first Stuart, and which since then had constantly kept alongside the throne, sometimes its support, sometimes its enemy, envying every great house, for greatness made it uneasy, but above all envious of the house of Hamilton, which, if not its equal, was at any rate after itself the next most powerful.

During the whole reign of James V, thanks to the hatred which the king bore them, the Douglases had: not only lost all their influence, but had also been exiled to England. This hatred was on account of their having seized the guardianship of the young prince and kept him prisoner till he was fifteen. Then, with the help of one of his pages, James V had escaped from Falkland, and had reached Stirling, whose governor was in his interests. Scarcely was he safe in the castle than he made proclamation that any Douglas who should approach within a dozen miles of it would be prosecuted for high treason. This was not all: he obtained a decree from Parliament, declaring them guilty of felony, and condemning them to exile; they remained proscribed, then, during the king's lifetime, and returned to Scotland only upon his death. The result was that, although they had been recalled about the throne, and though, thanks to the past influence of Murray, who, one remembers, was a Douglas on the mother's side, they filled the most important posts there, they had not forgiven to the daughter the enmity borne them by the father.

This was why James Douglas, chancellor as he was, and consequently entrusted with the execution of the laws, put himself at the head of a conspiracy which had for its aim the violation of all laws; human and divine.

Douglas's first idea had been to treat Rizzio as the favourites of James III had been treated at the Bridge of Lauder—that is to say, to make a show of having a trial and to hang him afterwards. But such a death did not suffice for Darnley's vengeance; as above everything he wished to punish the queen in Rizzio's person, he exacted that the murder should take place in her presence.

Douglas associated with himself Lord Ruthven, an idle and dissolute sybarite, who under the circumstances promised to push his devotion so far as to wear a cuirass; then, sure of this important accomplice, he busied himself with finding other agents.

However, the plot was not woven with such secrecy but that something of it transpired; and Rizzio received several warnings that he despised. Sir James Melville, among others, tried every means to make him understand the perils a stranger ran who enjoyed such absolute confidence in a wild, jealous court like that of Scotland. Rizzio received these hints as if resolved not to apply them to himself; and Sir James Melville, satisfied that he had done enough to ease his conscience, did not insist further. Then a French priest, who had a reputation as a clever astrologer, got himself admitted to Rizzio, and warned him that the stars predicted that he was in deadly peril, and that he should beware of a certain bastard above all. Rizzio replied that from the day when he had been honoured with his sovereign's confidence, he had sacrificed in advance his life to his position; that since that time, however, he had had occasion to notice that in general the Scotch were ready to threaten but slow to act; that, as to the bastard referred to, who was doubtless the Earl of Murray, he would take care that he should never enter Scotland far enough for his sword to reach him, were it as long as from Dumfries to Edinburgh; which in other words was as much as to say that Murray should remain exiled in England for life, since Dumfries was one of the principal frontier towns.

Meanwhile the conspiracy proceeded, and Douglas and Ruthven, having collected their accomplices and taken their measures, came to Darnley to finish the compact. As the price of the bloody service they rendered the king, they exacted from him a promise to obtain the pardon of Murray and the nobles compromised with him in the affair of the "run in every sense". Darnley granted all they asked of him, and a messenger was sent to Murray to inform him of the expedition in preparation, and to invite him to hold himself in readiness to reenter Scotland at the first notice he should receive. Then, this point settled, they made Darnley sign a paper in which he acknowledged himself the author and chief of the enterprise. The other assassins were the Earl of Morton, the Earl of Ruthven, George Douglas the bastard of Angus, Lindley, and Andrew, Carew. The remainder were soldiers, simple murderers' tools, who did not even know what was afoot. Darnley reserved it for himself to appoint the time.

Two days after these conditions were agreed upon, Darnley having been notified that the queen was alone with Rizzio, wished to make himself sure of the degree of her favour enjoyed by the minister. He accordingly went to her apartment by a little door of which he always kept the key upon him; but though the key turned in the lock, the door did not open. Then Darnley knocked, announcing himself; but such was the contempt into which he had fallen with the queen, that Mary left him outside, although, supposing she had been alone with Rizzio, she would have had time to send him away. Darnley, driven to extremities by this, summoned Morton, Ruthven, Lennox, Lindley, and Douglas's bastard, and fixed the assassination of Rizzio for two days later.

They had just completed all the details, and had distributed the parts that each must play in this bloody tragedy, when suddenly, and at the moment when they least expected it, the door opened and, Mary Stuart appeared on the threshold.

"My lords," said she, "your holding these secret counsels is useless. I am informed of your plots, and with God's help I shall soon apply a remedy".

With these words, and before the conspirators hid had time to collect themselves, she shut the door again, and vanished like a passing but threatening vision. All remained thunderstruck. Morton was the first to find his tongue.

"My lords," said he, "this is a game of life and death, and the winner will not be the cleverest or the strongest, but the readiest. If we do not destroy this man, we are lost. We must strike him down, this very evening, not the day after to-morrow."

Everyone applauded, even Ruthven, who, still pale and

feverish from riotous living, promised not to be behindhand. The only point changed, on Morton's suggestion, was that the murder should take place next day; for, in the opinion of all, not less than a day's interval was needed to collect the minor conspirators, who numbered not less than five hundred.

The next day, which was Saturday, March 9th, 1566, Mary Stuart, who had inherited from her father, James V, a dislike of ceremony and the need of liberty, had invited to supper with her six persons, Rizzio among the number. Darnley, informed of this in the morning, immediately gave notice of it to the conspirators, telling them that he himself would let them into the palace between six and seven o'clock in the evening. The conspirators replied that they would be in readiness.

The morning had been dark and stormy, as nearly all the first days of spring are in Scotland, and towards evening the snow and wind redoubled in depth and violence. So Mary had remained shut up with Rizzio, and Darnley, who had gone to the secret door several times, could hear the sound of instruments and the voice of the favourite, who was singing those sweet melodies which have come down to our time, and which Edinburgh people still attribute to him. These songs were for Mary a reminder of her stay in France, where the artists in the train of the Medicis had already brought echoes from Italy; but for Darnley they were an insult, and each time he had withdrawn strengthened in his design.

At the appointed time, the conspirators, who had been given the password during the day, knocked at the palace gate, and were received there so much the more easily that Darnley himself, wrapped in a great cloak, awaited them at the postern by which they were admitted. The five hundred soldiers immediately stole into an inner courtyard, where they placed themselves under some sheds, as much to keep themselves from the cold as that they might not be seen on the snow-covered ground. A brightly lighted window looked into this courtyard; it was that of the queen's study: at the first signal give them from this window, the soldiers were to break in the door and go to the help of the chief conspirators.

These instructions given, Darnley led Morton, Ruthven, Lennox, Lindley, Andrew Carew, and Douglas's bastard into the room adjoining the study, and only separated from it by a tapestry hanging before the door. From there one could overhear all that was being said, and at a single bound fall upon the guests.

Darnley left them in this room, enjoining silence; then, giving them as a signal to enter the moment when they should hear him cry, "To me, Douglas!" he went round by the secret passage, so that seeing him come in by his usual door the queen's suspicions might not be roused by his unlooked-for visit.

Mary was at supper with six persons, having, say de Thou and Melville, Rizzio seated on her right; while, on the contrary, Carapden assures us that he was eating standing at a sideboard. The talk was gay and intimate; for all were giving themselves up to the ease one feels at being safe and warm, at a hospitable board, while the snow is beating against the windows and the wind roaring in the chimneys. Suddenly Mary, surprised that the most profound silence had succeeded to the lively and animated flow of words among her guests since the beginning of supper, and suspecting, from their glances, that the cause of their uneasiness was behind her, turned round and saw Darnley leaning on the back of her chair. The queen shuddered; for although her husband was smiling when looking at Rizzio, this smile lead assumed such a strange expression that it was clear that something terrible was about to happen. At the same moment, Mary heard in the next room a heavy, dragging step drew near the cabinet, then the tapestry was raised, and Lord Ruthven, in armour of which he could barely support the weight, pale as a ghost, appeared on the threshold, and, drawing his sword in silence, leaned upon it.

The queen thought he was delirious.

"What do you want, my lord?" she said to him; "and why do you come to the palace like this?"

"Ask the king, madam," replied Ruthven in an indistinct voice. "It is for him to answer."

"Explain, my lord," Mary demanded, turning again towards Darnley; "what does such a neglect of ordinary propriety mean?"

"It means, madam," returned Darnley, pointing to Rizzio, "that that man must leave here this very minute."

"That man is mine, my lord," Mary said, rising proudly, "and consequently takes orders only from me."

"To me, Douglas!" cried Darnley.

At these words, the conspirators, who for some moments had drawn nearer Ruthven, fearing, so changeable was Darnley's character, lest he had brought them in vain and would not dare to utter the signal—at these words, the conspirators rushed into the room with such haste that they overturned the table. Then David Rizzio, seeing that it was he alone they wanted, threw himself on his knees behind the queen, seizing the hem of her robe and crying in Italian, "Giustizia! giustizia!" Indeed, the queen, true to her character, not allowing herself to be intimidated by this terrible irruption, placed herself in front of Rizzio and sheltered him behind her Majesty. But she counted too much on the respect of a nobility accustomed to struggle hand to hand with its kings for five centuries. Andrew Carew held a dagger to her breast and threatened to kill her if she insisted on defending any longer him whose death was resolved upon. Then Darnley, without consideration for the queen's pregnancy, seized her round the waist and bore her away from Rizzio, who remained on his knees pale and trembling, while Douglas's bastard, confirming the prediction of the astrologer who had warned Rizzio to beware of a certain bastard, drawing the king's own dagger, plunged it into the breast of the minister, who fell wounded, but not dead. Morton immediately took him by the feet and dragged him from the cabinet into the larger room, leaving on the floor that long track of blood which is still shown there; then, arrived there, each rushed upon him as upon a quarry, and set upon the corpse, which they stabbed in fifty-six places. Meanwhile Darnley held the queen, who, thinking that all was not over, did not cease crying for mercy. But Ruthven came back, paler than at first, and at Darnley's inquiry if Rizzio were dead, he nodded in the affirmative; then, as he could not bear further fatigue in his convalescent state, he sat down, although the queen, whom Darnley had at last released, remained standing on the same spot. At this Mary could not contain herself.

"My lord," cried she, "who has given you permission to sit down in my presence, and whence comes such insolence?"

"Madam," Ruthven answered, "I act thus not from insolence, but from weakness; for, to serve your husband, I have just taken more exercise than my doctors allow". Then turning round to a servant, "Give me a glass of wine," said he, showing Darnley his bloody dagger before putting it back in its sheath, "for here is the proof that I have well earned it". The servant obeyed, and Ruthven drained his glass with as much calmness as if he had just performed the most innocent act.

"My lord," the queen then said, taking a step towards him, "it may be that as I am a woman, in spite of my desire and my will, I never find an opportunity to repay you what you are doing to me; but," she added, energetically striking her womb with her hand, "he whom I bear there, and whose life you should have respected, since you respect my Majesty so little, will one day revenge me for all these insults". Then, with a gesture at once superb and threatening, she withdrew by Darnley's door, which she closed behind her.

At that moment a great noise was heard in the queen's

room. Huntly, Athol, and Bothwell, who, we are soon about to see, play such an important part in the sequel of this history, were supping together in another hall of the palace, when suddenly they had heard outcries and the clash of arms, so that they had run with all speed. When Athol, who came first, without knowing whose it was, struck against the dead body of Rizzio, which was stretched at the top of the staircase, they believed, seeing someone assassinated, that the lives of the king and queen were threatened, and they had drawn their swords to force the door that Morton was guarding. But directly Darnley understood what was going on, he darted from the cabinet, followed by Ruthven, and showing himself to the newcomers—

"My lords," he said, "the persons of the queen and myself are safe, and nothing has occurred here but by our orders. Withdraw, then; you will know more about it in time. As to him," he added, holding up Rizzio's head by the hair, whilst the bastard of Douglas lit up the face with a torch so that it could be recognised, "you see who it is, and whether it is worth your while to get into trouble for him".

And in fact, as soon as Huntly, Athol, and Bothwell had recognised the musician-minister, they sheathed their swords, and, having saluted the king, went away.

Mary had gone away with a single thought in her heart, vengeance. But she understood that she could not revenge herself at one and the same time on her husband and his companions: she set to work, then, with all the charms of her wit and beauty to detach the kind from his accomplices.

It was not a difficult task: when that brutal rage which often carried Darnley beyond all bounds was spent, he was frightened himself at the crime he had committed, and while the assassins, assembled by Murray, were resolving that he should have that greatly desired crown matrimonial, Darnley, as fickle as he was violent, and as cowardly as he was cruel, in Mary's very room, before the scarcely dried blood, made another compact, in which he engaged to deliver up his accomplices. Indeed, three days after the event that we have just related, the murderers learned a strange piece of news—that Darnley and Mary, accompanied by Lord Seyton, had escaped together from Holyrood Palace. Three days later still, a proclamation appeared, signed by Mary and dated from Dunbar, which summoned round the queen, in her own name and the king's, all the Scottish lords and barons, including those who had been compromised in the affair of the "run in every sense," to whom she not only granted full and complete pardon, but also restored her entire confidence. In this way she separated Murray's cause from that of Morton and the other assassins, who, in their turn, seeing that there was no longer any safety for them in Scotland, fled to England, where all the queen's enemies were always certain to find a warm welcome, in spite of the good relations which reigned in appearance between Mary and Elizabeth. As to Bothwell, who had wanted to oppose the assassination, he was appointed Warden of all the Marches of the Kingdom.

Unfortunately for her honour, Mary, always more the woman than the queen, while, on the contrary, Elizabeth was always more the queen than the woman, had no sooner regained her power than her first royal act was to exhume Rizzio, who had been quietly buried on the threshold of the chapel nearest Holyrood Palace, and to have him removed to the burial-place of the Scottish kings, compromising herself still more by the honours she paid him dead than by the favour she had granted him living.

Such an imprudent demonstration naturally led to fresh quarrels between Mary and Darnley: these quarrels were the more bitter that, as one can well understand, the reconciliation between the husband and wife, at least on the latter's side, had never been anything but a pretence; so that, feeling herself in a stronger position still on account of her pregnancy, she restrained herself no longer, and, leaving Darnley, she went from Dunbar to Edinburgh Castle, where on June 19th, 1566, three months after the assassination of Rizzio, she gave birth to a son who afterwards became James VI.

CHAPTER III

Directly she was delivered, Mary sent for James Melville, her usual envoy to Elizabeth, and charged him to convey this news to the Queen of England, and to beg her to be godmother to the royal child at the same time. On arriving in London, Melville immediately presented himself at the palace; but as there was a court ball, he could not see the queen, and contented himself with making known the reason for his journey to the minister Cecil, and with begging him to ask his mistress for an audience next day. Elizabeth was dancing in a quadrille at the moment when Cecil, approaching her, said in a low voice, "Queen Mary of Scotland has just given birth to a son". At these words she grew frightfully pale, and, looking about her with a bewildered air, and as if she were about to faint, she leaned against an arm-chair; then, soon, not being able to stand upright, she sat down, threw back her head, and plunged into a mournful reverie. Then one of the ladies of her court, breaking through the circle which had formed round the queen, approached her, ill at ease, and asked her of what she was thinking so sadly. "Ah! madam," Elizabeth replied impatiently, "do you not know that Mary Stuart has given birth to a son, while I am but a barren stock, who will die without offspring?"

Yet Elizabeth was too good a politician, in spite of her liability to be carried away by a first impulse, to compromise herself by a longer display of her grief. The ball was not discontinued on that account, and the interrupted quadrille was resumed and finished.

The next day, Melville had his audience. Elizabeth received him to perfection, assuring him of all the pleasure that the news he brought had caused her, and which, she said, had cured her of a complaint from which she had suffered for a fortnight. Melville replied that his mistress had hastened to acquaint her with her joy, knowing that she had no better friend; but he added that this joy had nearly cost Mary her life, so grievous had been her confinement. As he was returning to this point for the third time, with the object of still further increasing the queen of England's dislike to marriage—

"Be easy, Melville," Elizabeth answered him; "you need not insist upon it. I shall never marry; my kingdom takes the place of a husband for me, and my subjects are my children. When I am dead, I wish graven on my tombstone: 'Here lies Elizabeth, who reigned so many years, and who died a virgin.'"

Melville availed himself of this opportunity to remind Elizabeth of the desire she had shown to see Mary, three or four years before; but Elizabeth said, besides her country's affairs, which necessitated her presence in the heart of her possessions, she did not care, after all she had heard said of her rival's beauty, to expose herself to a comparison disadvantageous to her pride. She contented herself, then, with choosing as her proxy the Earl of Bedford, who set out with several other noblemen for Stirling Castle, where the young prince was christened with great pomp, and received the name of Charles James.

It was remarked that Darnley did not appear at this ceremony, and that his absence seemed to scandalise greatly the queen of England's envoy. On the contrary, James Hepburn, Earl of Bothwell, had the most important place there.

This was because, since the evening when Bothwell, at Mary's cries, had run to oppose the murder of Rizzio, he had made great way in the queen's favour; to her party he himself appeared to be really attached, to the exclusion of the two others, the king's and the Earl of Murray's. Bothwell was already thirty-five years old, head of the powerful family of Hepburn, which had great influence in East Lothian and the county of Berwick; for the rest, violent, rough, given to every kind of debauchery, and capable of anything to satisfy an ambition that he did not even give himself the trouble to hide. In his youth he had been reputed courageous, but for long he had had no serious opportunity to draw the sword.

If the king's authority had been shaken by Rizzio's influence, it was entirely upset by Bothwell's. The great nobles, following the favourite's example, no longer rose in the presence of Darnley, and ceased little by little to treat him as their equal: his retinue was cut down, his silver plate taken from him, and some officers who remained about him made him buy their services with the most bitter vexations. As for the queen, she no longer even took the trouble to conceal her dislike for him, avoiding him without consideration, to such a degree that one day when she had gone with Bothwell to Alway, she left there again immediately, because Darnley came to join her. The king, however, still had patience; but a fresh imprudence of Mary's at last led to the terrible catastrophe that, since the queen's liaison with Bothwell, some had already foreseen.

Towards the end of the month of October, 1566, while the queen was holding a court of justice at Jedburgh, it was announced to her that Bothwell, in trying to seize a malefactor called John Elliot of Park, had been badly wounded in the hand; the queen, who was about to attend the council, immediately postponed the sitting till next day, and, having ordered a horse to be saddled, she set out for Hermitage Castle, where Bothwell was living, and covered the distance at a stretch, although it was twenty miles, and she had to go across woods, marshes, and rivers; then, having remained some hours tete-a-tete with him, she set out again with the same sped for Jedburgh, to which she returned in the night.

Although this proceeding had made a great deal of talk, which was inflamed still more by the queen's enemies, who chiefly belonged to the Reformed religion, Darnley did not hear of it till nearly two months afterwards—that is to say, when Bothwell, completely recovered, returned with the queen to Edinburgh.

Then Darnley thought that he ought not to put up any longer with such humiliations. But as, since his treason to his accomplices, he had not found in all Scotland a noble who would have drawn the sword for him, he resolved to go and seek the Earl of Lennox, his father, hoping that through his influence he could rally the malcontents, of whom there were a great number since Bothwell had been in favour. Unfortunately, Darnley, indiscreet and imprudent as usual, confided this plan to some of his officers, who warned Bothwell of their master's intention. Bothwell did not seem to oppose the journey in any way; but Darnley was scarcely a mile from Edinburgh when he felt violent pains none the less, he continued his road, and arrived very ill at Glasgow. He immediately sent for a celebrated doctor, called James Abrenets, who found his body covered with pimples, and declared without any hesitation that he had been poisoned. However, others, among them Walter Scott, state that this illness was nothing else than smallpox.

Whatever it may have been, the queen, in the presence of the danger her husband ran, appeared to forget her resentment, and at the risk of what might prove troublesome to herself, she went to Darnley, after sending her doctor in advance. It is true that if one is to believe in the following letters, dated from Glasgow, which Mary is accused of having written to Bothwell, she knew the illness with which he was attacked too well to fear infection. As these letters are little known, and seem to us very singular we transcribe them here; later we shall tell how they fell into the power of the Confederate lords, and from their hands passed into Elizabeth's, who, quite delighted, cried on receiving them, "God's death, then I hold her life and honour in my hands!"

FIRST LETTER

"When I set out from the place where I had left my heart, judge in what a condition I was, poor body without a soul: besides, during the whole of dinner I have not spoken to anyone, and no one has dared to approach me, for it was easy to see that there was something amiss. When I arrived within a league of the town, the Earl of Lennox sent me one of his gentlemen to make me his compliments, and to excuse himself for not having come in person; he has caused me to be informed, moreover, that he did not dare to present himself before me after the reprimand that I gave Cunningham. This gentleman begged me, as if of his own accord, to examine his master's conduct, to ascertain if my suspicions were well founded. I have replied to him that fear was an incurable disease, that the Earl of Lennox would not be so agitated if his conscience reproached him with nothing, and that if some hasty words had escaped me, they were but just reprisals for the letter he had written me.

"None of the inhabitants visited me, which makes me think they are all in his interests; besides, they speak of him very favourably, as well as of his son. The king sent for Joachim yesterday, and asked him why I did not lodge with him, adding that my presence would soon cure him, and asked me also with what object I had come: if it were to be reconciled with him; if you were here; if I had taken Paris and Gilbert as secretaries, and if I were still resolved to dismiss Joseph? I do not know who has given him such accurate information. There is nothing, down to the marriage of Sebastian, with which he has not made himself acquainted.

I have asked him the meaning of one of his letters, in which he complains of the cruelty of certain people. He replied that he was—stricken, but that my presence caused him so much joy that he thought he should die of it. He reproached me several times for being dreamy; I left him to go to supper; he begged me to return: I went back. Then he told me the story of his illness, and that he wished to make a will leaving me everything, adding that I was a little the cause of his trouble, and that he attributed it to my coldness. 'You ask me,' added he, 'who are the people of whom I complain: it is of you, cruel one, of you, whom I have never been able to appease by my tears and my repentance. I know that I have offended you, but not on the matter that you reproach me with: I have also offended some of your subjects, but that you have forgiven me. I am young, and you say that I always relapse into my faults; but cannot a young man like me, destitute of experience, gain it also, break his promises, repent directly, and in time improve? If you will forgive me yet once more, I will promise to offend you never again. All the favour I ask of you is that we should live together like husband and wife, to have but one bed and one board: if you are inflexible, I shall never rise again from here. I entreat you, tell me your decision: God alone knows what I suffer, and that because I occupy myself with you only, because I love and adore only you. If I have offended you sometimes, you must bear the reproach; for when someone offends me, if it were granted me to complain to you, I should not confide my griefs to others; but when we are on bad terms, I am obliged to keep them to myself, and that maddens me.'

"He then urged me strongly to stay with him and lodge in his house; but I excused myself, and replied that he ought to be purged, and that he could not be, conveniently, at Glasgow; then he told me that he knew I had brought a letter for him, but that he would have preferred to make the journey with me. He believed, I think, that I meant to send him to some prison: I replied that I should take him to Craigmiller, that he would find doctors there, that I should remain near him, and that we should be within reach of seeing my son. He has answered that he will go where I wish to take him, provided that I grant him what he has asked. He does not, however, wish to be seen by anyone.

"He has told me more than a hundred pretty things that I cannot repeat to you, and at which you yourself would be surprised: he did not want to let me go; he wanted to make me sit up with him all night. As for me, I pretended to believe everything, and I seemed to interest myself really in him. Besides, I have never seen him so small and humble; and if I had not known how easily his heart overflows, and how mine is impervious to every other arrow than those with which you have wounded it, I believe that I should have allowed myself to soften; but lest that should alarm you, I would die rather than give up what I have promised you. As for you, be sure to act in the same way towards those traitors who will do all they can to separate you from me. I believe that all those people have been cast in the same mould: this one always has a tear in his eye; he bows down before everyone, from the greatest to the smallest; he wishes to interest them in his favour, and make himself pitied. His father threw up blood to-day through the nose and mouth; think what these symptoms mean. I have not seen him yet, for he keeps to the house. The king wants me to feed him myself; he won't eat unless I do. But, whatever I may do, you will be deceived by it no more than I shall be deceiving myself. We are united, you and I, to two kinds of very detestable people [Mary means Miss Huntly, Bothwell's wife, whom he repudiated, at the king's death, to marry the queen.]: that hell may sever these knots then, and that heaven may form better ones, that nothing can break, that it may make of us the most tender and faithful couple that ever was; there is the profession of faith in which I would die.

"Excuse my scrawl: you must guess more than the half of it, but I know no help for this. I am obliged to write to you hastily while everyone is asleep here: but be easy, I take infinite pleasure in my watch; for I cannot sleep like the others, not being able to sleep as I would like—that is to say, in your arms.

"I am going to get into bed; I shall finish my letter tomorrow: I have too many things to tell to you, the night is too far advanced: imagine my despair. It is to you I am writing, it is of myself that I converse with you, and I am obliged to make an end.

"I cannot prevent myself, however, from filling up hastily the rest of my paper. Cursed be the crazy creature who torments me so much! Were it not for him, I could talk to you of more agreeable things: he is not greatly changed; and yet he has taken a great deal o f %t. But he has nearly killed me with the fetid smell of his breath; for now his is still worse than your cousin's: you guess that this is a fresh reason for my not approaching him; on the contrary, I go away as far as I can, and sit on a chair at the foot of his bed.

"Let us see if I forget anything:

"His father's messenger on the road;

The question about Joachim;

The-state of my house;

The people of my suite;

Subject of my arrival;

Joseph;

Conversation between him and me;

His desire to please me and his repentance;

The explanation of his letter;

Mr. Livingston.

"Ah! I was forgetting that. Yesterday Livingston during supper told de Rere in a low voice to drink to the health of one I knew well, and to beg me to do him the honour. After supper, as I was leaning on his shoulder near the fire, he said to me, 'Is it not true that there are visits very agreeable for those who pay them and those who receive them? But, however satisfied they seem with your arrival, I challenge their delight to equal the grief of one whom you have left alone to-day, and who will never be content till he sees you again.' I asked him of whom he wished to speak to me. He then answered me by pressing my arm: 'Of one of those who have not followed you; and among those it is easy for you to guess of whom I want to speak.'

"I have worked till two o'clock at the bracelet; I have enclosed a little key which is attached by two strings: it is not as well worked as I should like, but I have not had time to make it better; I will make you a finer one on the first occasion. Take care that it is not seen on you; for I have worked at it before everyone, and it would be recognised to a certainty.

"I always return, in spite of myself, to the frightful attempt that you advise. You compel me to concealments, and above all to treacheries that make me shudder; I would rather die, believe me, than do such things; for it makes my heart bleed. He does not want to follow me unless I promise him to have the selfsame bed and board with him as before, and not to abandon him so often. If I consent to it, he says he will do all I wish, and will follow me everywhere; but he has begged me to put off my departure for two days. I have pretended to agree to all he wishes; but I have told him not to speak of our reconciliation to anyone, for fear it should make some lords uneasy. At last I shall take him everywhere I wish.... Alas! I have never deceived anyone; but what would I not do to please you? Command, and whatever happens, I shall obey. But see yourself if one could not contrive some secret means in the shape of a remedy. He must purge himself at Craigmiller and take baths there; he will be some days without going out. So far as I can see, he is very uneasy; but he has great trust in what I tell him: however, his confidence does not go so far as to allow him to open his mind to me. If you like, I will tell him every thing: I can have no pleasure in deceiving someone who is trusting. However, it will be just as you wish: do not esteem me the less for that. It is you advised it; never would vengeance have taken me so far. Sometimes he attacks me in a very sensitive place, and he touches me to the quick when he tells me that his crimes are known, but that every day greater ones are committed that one uselessly attempts to hide, since all crimes, whatsoever they be, great or small, come to men's knowledge and form the common subject of their discourse. He adds sometimes, in speaking to me of Madame de Rere, 'I wish her services may do you honour.' He has assured me that many people thought, and that he thought himself, that I was not my own mistress; this is doubtless because I had rejected the conditions he offered me. Finally, it is certain that he is very uneasy about you know what, and that he even suspects that his life is aimed at. He is in despair whenever the conversation turns on you, Livingston, and my brother. However, he says neither good nor ill of absent people; but, on the contrary, he always avoids speaking of them. His father keeps to the house: I have not seen him yet. A number of the Hamiltons are here, and accompany me everywhere; all the friends of the other one follow me each time I go to see him. He has begged me to be at his rising to-morrow. My messenger will tell you the rest.

"Burn my letter: there would be danger in keeping it. Besides, it is hardly worth the trouble, being filled only with dark thoughts.

"As for you, do not be offended if I am sad and uneasy to-day, that to please you I rise above honour, remorse, and dangers. Do not take in bad part what I tell you, and do not listen to the malicious explanations of your wife's brother; he is a knave whom you ought not to hear to the prejudice of the most tender and most faithful mistress that ever was. Above all, do not allow yourself to be moved by that woman: her sham tears are nothing in comparison with the real tears that I shed, and with what love and constancy make me suffer at succeeding her; it is for that alone that in spite of myself I betray all those who could cross my love. God have mercy on me, and send you all the prosperity that a humble and tender friend who awaits from you soon another reward wishes you. It is very late; but it is always with regret that I lay down my pen when I write to you; however, I shall not end my letter until I shall have kissed your hands. Forgive me that it is so ill-written: perhaps I do so expressly that you may be obliged to re-read it several times: I have transcribed hastily what I had written down on my tablets, and my paper has given out. Remember a tender friend, and write to her often: love me as tenderly as I love you, and remember:

"Madame de Rere's words;

The English;

His mother;

The Earl of Argyll;

The Earl of Bothwell;

The Edinburgh dwelling."

SECOND LETTER

"It seems that you have forgotten me during your absence, so much the more that you had promised me, at setting out, to let me know in detail everything fresh that should happen. The hope of receiving your news was giving me almost as much delight as your return could have brought me: you have put it off longer than you promised me. As for me, although you do not write, I play my part always. I shall take him to Craigmiller on Monday, and he will spend the whole of Wednesday there. On that day I shall go to Edinburgh to be bled there, unless you arrange otherwise at least. He is more cheerful than usual, and he is better than ever.

"He says everything he can to persuade me that he loves me; he has a thousand attentions for me, and he anticipates me in everything: all that is so pleasant for me, that I never go to him but the pain in my side comes on again, his company weighs on me so much. If Paris brought me what I asked him, I should be soon cured. If you have not yet returned when I go you know where, write to me, I beg you, and tell me what you wish me to do; for if you do not manage things prudently, I foresee that the whole burden will fall on me: look into everything and weigh the affair maturely. I send you my letter by Beaton, who will set out the day which has been assigned to Balfour. It only remains for me to beg you to inform me of your journey.

"Glasgow, this Saturday morning."

THIRD LETTER

"I stayed you know where longer than I should have done,

if it had not been to get from him something that the bearer of these presents will tell you it was a good opportunity for covering up our designs: I have promised him to bring the person you know to-morrow. Look after the rest, if you think fit. Alas! I have failed in our agreement, for you have forbidden me to write to you, or to despatch a messenger to you. However, I do not intend to offend you: if you knew with what fears I am agitated, you would not have yourself so many doubts and suspicions. But I take them in good part, persuaded as I am that they have no other cause than love—love that I esteem more than anything on earth.

"My feelings and my favours are to me sure warrants for that love, and answer to me for your heart; my trust is entire on this head: but explain yourself, I entreat you, and open your soul to me; otherwise, I shall fear lest, by the fatality of my star, and by the too fortunate influence of the stars on women less tender and less faithful than I, I may be supplanted in your heart as Medea was in Jason's; not that I wish to compare you to a lover as unfortunate as Jason, and to parallel myself with a monster like Medea, although you have enough influence over me to force me to resemble her each time our love exacts it, and that it concerns me to keep your heart, which belongs to me, and which belongs to me only. For I name as belonging to me what I have purchased with the tender and constant love with which I have burned for you, a love more alive to-day than ever, and which will end only with my life; a love, in short, which makes me despise both the dangers and the remorse which will be perhaps its sad sequel. As the price of this sacrifice, I ask you but one favour, it is to remember a spot not far from here: I do not exact that you should keep your promise to-morrow; but I want to see you to disperse your suspicions. I ask of God only one thing: it is that He should make you read my heart, which is less mine than yours, and that He should guard you from every ill, at least during my life: this life is dear to me only in so far as it pleases you, and as I please you myself. I am going to bed: adieu; give me your news to-morrow morning; for I shall be uneasy till I have it. Like a bird escaped from its cage, or the turtle-dove which has lost her mate, I shall be alone, weeping your absence, short as it may be. This letter, happier than I, will go this evening where I cannot go, provided that the messenger does not find you asleep, as I fear. I have not dared to write it in the presence of Joseph, of Sebastian, and of Joachim, who had only just left me when I began it."

Thus, as one sees, and always supposing these letters to be genuine, Mary had conceived for Bothwell one of those mad passions, so much the stronger in the women who are a prey to them, that one the less understands what could have inspired them. Bothwell was no longer young, Bothwell was not handsome, and yet Mary sacrificed for him a young husband, who was considered one of the handsomest men of his century. It was like a kind of enchantment. Darnley, the sole obstacle to the union, had been already condemned for a long time, if not by Mary, at least by Bothwell; then, as his strong constitution had conquered the poison, another kind of death was sought for.

The queen, as she announces in her letter to Bothwell, had refused to bring back Darnley with her, and had returned alone to Edinburgh. Arrived there, she gave orders for the king to be moved, in his turn, in a litter; but instead of taking him to Stirling or Holyrood, she decided to lodge him in the abbey of the Kirk of Field. The king made some objections when he knew of this arrangement; however, as he had no power to oppose it, he contented himself with complaining of the solitude of the dwelling assigned him; but the queen made answer that she could not receive him at that moment, either at Holyrood or at Stirling, for fear, if his illness were infectious, lest he might give it to his son: Darnley was then obliged to make the best of the abode allotted him.

It was an isolated abbey, and little calculated by its position to dissipate the fears that the king entertained; for it was situated between two ruined churches and two cemeteries: the only house, which was distant about a shot from a cross-bow, belonged to the Hamiltons, and as they were Darnley's mortal enemies the neighbourhood was none the more reassuring: further, towards the north, rose some wretched huts, called the "Thieves' cross-roads". In going round his new residence, Darnley noticed that three holes, each large enough for a man to get through, had been made in the walls; he asked that these holes, through which ill-meaning persons could get in, should be stopped up: it was promised that masons should be sent; but nothing was done, and the holes remained open.

The day after his arrival at Kirk of Field, the king saw a

light in that house near his which he believed deserted; next day he asked Alexander Durham whence it came, and he heard that the Archbishop of St. Andrew's had left his palace in Edinburgh and had housed there since the preceding evening, one didn't know why: this news still further increased the king's uneasiness; the Archbishop of St. Andrew's was one of his most declared enemies.

The king, little by little abandoned by all his servants lived on the first floor of an isolated pavilion, having about him only this same Alexander Durham, whom we have mentioned already, and who was his valet. Darnley, who had quite a special friendship for him, and who besides, as we have said, feared some attack on his life at every moment, had made him move his bed into his own apartment, so that both were sleeping in the same room.

On the night of the 8th February, Darnley awoke Durham: he thought he heard footsteps in the apartment beneath him. Durham rose, took a sword in one hand, a taper in the other, and went down to the ground floor; but although Darnley was quite certain he had not been deceived, Durham came up again a moment after, saying he had seen no one.

The morning of the next day passed without bringing anything fresh. The queen was marrying one of her servants named Sebastian: he was an Auvergnat whom she had brought with her from France, and whom she liked very much. However, as the king sent word that he had not seen her for two days, she left the wedding towards six o'clock in the evening, and came to pay him a visit, accompanied by the Countess of Argyll and the Countess of Huntly. While she was there, Durham, in preparing his bed, set fire to his palliasse, which was burned as well as a part of the mattress; so that, having thrown them out of the window all in flames, for fear lest the fire should reach the rest of the furniture, he found himself without a bed, and asked permission to return to the town to sleep; but Darnley, who remembered his terror the night before, and who was surprised at the promptness that had made Durham throw all his bedding out of the window, begged him not to go away, offering him one of his mattresses, or even to take him into his own bed. However, in spite of this offer, Durham insisted, saying that he felt unwell, and that he should like to see a doctor the same evening. So the queen interceded for Durham, and promised Darnley to send him another valet to spend the night with him: Darnley was then obliged to yield, and, making Mary repeat that she would send him someone, he gave Durham leave for that evening. At that moment Paris, of whom the queen speaks in her letters, came in: he was a young Frenchman who had been in Scotland for some years, and who, after having served with Bothwell and Seyton, was at present with the queen. Seeing him, she got up, and as Darnley still wished to keep her—

"Indeed, my lord, it is impossible," said she, "to come and see you. I have left this poor Sebastian's wedding, and I must return to it; for I promised to came masked to his ball."

The king dared not insist; he only reminded her of the promise that she had made to send him a servant:

Mary renewed it yet once again, and went away with her attendants. As for Durham, he had set out the moment he received permission.

It was nine o'clock in the evening. Darnley, left alone, carefully shut the doors within, and retired to rest, though in readiness to rise to let in the servant who should come to spend the night with him. Scarcely was he in bed than the same noise that he had heard the night before recommenced; this time Darnley listened with all the attention fear gives, and soon he had no longer any doubt but that several men were walking about beneath him. It was useless to call, it was dangerous to go out; to wait was the only course that remained to the king. He made sure again that the doors were well fastened, put his sword under his pillow, extinguished his lamp for fear the light might betray him, and awaited in silence for his servant's arrival; but the hours passed away, and the servant did not come. At one o'clock in the morning, Bothwell, after having talked some while with the queen, in the presence of the captain of the guard, returned home to change his dress; after some minutes, he came out wrapped up in the large cloak of a German hussar, went through the guard-house, and had the castle gate opened. Once outside, he took his way with all speed to Kirk of Field, which he entered by the opening in the wall: scarcely had he made a step in the garden than he met James Balfour, governor of the castle.

"Well," he said to him, "how far have we got?

"Everything is ready," replied Balfour, "and we were

waiting for you to set fire to the fuse". "That is well," Bothwell answered—"but first I want to make sure that he is in his room."

At these words, Bothwell opened the pavilion door with a false key, and, having groped his way up the stairs; he went to listen at Darnley's door. Darnley, hearing no further noise, had ended by going to sleep; but he slept with a jerky breathing which pointed to his agitation. Little mattered it to Bothwell what kind of sleep it was, provided that he was really in his room. He went down again in silence, then, as he had come up, and taking a lantern from one of the conspirators, he went himself into the lower room to see if everything was in order: this room was full of barrels of powder, and a fuse ready prepared wanted but a spark to set the whole on fire. Bothwell withdrew, then, to the end of the garden with Balfour, David, Chambers, and three or four others, leaving one man to ignite the fuse. In a moment this man rejoined them.

There ensued some minutes of anxiety, during which the five men looked at one another in silence and as if afraid of themselves; then, seeing that nothing exploded, Bothwell impatiently turned round to the engineer, reproaching him for having, no doubt through fear, done his work badly. He assured his master that he was certain everything was all right, and as Bothwell, impatient, wanted to return to the house himself, to make sure, he offered to go back and see how things stood. In fact, he went back to the pavilion, and, putting his head through a kind of air-hole, he saw the fuse, which was still burning. Some seconds afterwards, Bothwell saw him come running back, making a sign that all was going well; at the same moment a frightful report was heard, the pavilion was blown to pieces, the town and the firth were lit up with a clearness exceeding the brightest daylight; then everything fell back into night, and the silence was broken only by the fall of stones and joists, which came down as fast as hail in a hurricane.

Next day the body of the king was found in a garden in the neighbourhood: it had been saved from the action of the fire by the mattresses on which he was lying, and as, doubtless, in his terror he had merely thrown himself on his bed wrapped in his dressing-gown and in his slippers, and as he was found thus, without his slippers, which were flung some paces away, it was believed that he had been first strangled, then carried there; but the most probable version was that the murderers simply relied upon powder—an auxiliary sufficiently powerful in itself for them to have no fear it would fail them.

Was the queen an accomplice or not? No one has ever known save herself, Bothwell, and God; but, yes or no, her conduct, imprudent this time as always, gave the charge her enemies brought against her, if not substance, at least an appearance of truth. Scarcely had she heard the news than she gave orders that the body should be brought to her, and, having had it stretched out upon a bench, she looked at it with more curiosity than sadness; then the corpse, embalmed, was placed the same evening, without pomp, by the side of

Rizzio's.

Scottish ceremonial prescribes for the widows of kings retirement for forty days in a room entirely closed to the light of day: on the twelfth day Mary had the windows opened, and on the fifteenth set out with Bothwell for Seaton, a country house situated five miles from the capital, where the French ambassador, Ducroc, went in search of her, and made her remonstrances which decided her to return to Edinburgh; but instead of the cheers which usually greeted her coming, she was received by an icy silence, and a solitary woman in the crowd called out, "God treat her as she deserves!"

The names of the murderers were no secret to the people. Bothwell having brought a splendid coat which was too large for him to a tailor, asking him to remake it to his measure, the man recognised it as having belonged to the king. "That's right," said he; "it is the custom for the executioner to inherit from the-condemned". Meanwhile, the Earl of Lennox, supported by the people's murmurs, loudly demanded justice for his son's death, and came forward as the accuser of his murderers. The queen was then obliged, to appease paternal clamour and public resentment, to command the Earl of Argyll, the Lord Chief Justice of the kingdom, to make investigations; the same day that this order was given, a proclamation was posted up in the streets of Edinburgh, in which the queen promised two thousand pounds sterling to whoever would make known the king's murderers. Next day, wherever this letter had been affixed, another placard was found, worded thus:

"As it has been proclaimed that those who should make known the king's murderers should have two thousand pounds sterling, I, who have made a strict search, affirm that the authors of the murder are the Earl of Bothwell, James Balfour, the priest of Flisk, David, Chambers, Blackmester, Jean Spens, and the queen herself."

This placard was torn down; but, as usually happens, it had already been read by the entire population.

The Earl of Lennox accused Bothwell, and public opinion, which also accused him, seconded the earl with such violence, that Mary was compelled to bring him to trial: only every precaution was taken to deprive the prosecutor of the power of convicting the accused. On the 28th March, the Earl of Lennox received notice that the 12th April was fixed for the trial: he was granted a fortnight to collect decisive proofs against the most powerful man in all Scotland; but the Earl of Lennox, judging that this trial was a mere mockery, did not appear. Bothwell, on the contrary, presented himself at the court, accompanied by five thousand partisans and two hundred picked fusiliers, who guarded the doors directly he had entered; so that he seemed to be rather a king who is about to violate the law than an accused who comes to submit to it. Of course there happened what was certain to happen—that is to say, the jury acquitted Bothwell of the crime of which everyone, the judges included, knew him to be guilty.

The day of the trial, Bothwell had this written challenge placarded:

"Although I am sufficiently cleared of the murder of the king, of which I have been falsely accused, yet, the better to prove my innocence, I am, ready to engage in combat with whomsoever will dare to maintain that I have killed the king."

The day after, this reply appeared:

"I accept the challenge, provided that you select neutral ground."

However, judgment had been barely given, when rumours of a marriage between the queen and the Earl of Bothwell were abroad. However strange and however mad this marriage, the relations of the two lovers were so well known that no one doubted but that it was true. But as everyone submitted to Bothwell, either through fear or through ambition, two men only dared to protest beforehand against this union: the one was Lord Herries, and the other James Melville.

Mary was at Stirling when Lord Herries, taking advantage of Bothwell's momentary absence, threw himself at her feet, imploring her not to lose her honour by marrying her husband's murderer, which could not fail to convince those who still doubted it that she was his accomplice. But the queen, instead of thanking Herries for this devotion, seemed very much surprised at his boldness, and scornfully signing to him to rise, she coldly replied that her heart was silent as regarded the Earl of Bothwell, and that, if she should ever re-marry, which was not probable, she would neither forget what she owed to her people nor what she owed to herself.

Melville did not allow himself to be discouraged by this

experience, and pretended, to have received a letter that one of his friends, Thomas Bishop, had written him from England. He showed this letter to the queen; but at the first lines Mary recognised the style, and above all the friendship of her ambassador, and giving the letter to the Earl of Livingston, who was present, "There is a very singular letter," said she. "Read it. It is quite in Melvine's manner."

Livingston glanced through the letter, but had scarcely read the half of it when he took Melville by the hand, and drawing him into the embrasure of a window,

"My dear Melville," said he, "you were certainly mad when you just now imparted this letter to the queen: as soon as the Earl of Bothwell gets wind of it, and that will not be long, he will have you assassinated. You have behaved like an honest man, it is true; but at court it is better to behave as a clever man. Go away, then, as quickly as possible; it is I who recommend it."

Melville did not require to be told twice, and stayed away for a week. Livingston was not mistaken: scarcely had Bothwell returned to the queen than he knew all that had passed. He burst out into curses against Melville, and sought for him everywhere; but he could not find him.

This beginning of opposition, weak as it was, none the less disquieted Bothwell, who, sure of Mary's love, resolved to make short work of things. Accordingly, as the queen was returning from Stirling to Edinburgh some days after the scenes we have just related, Bothwell suddenly appeared at the Bridge of Grammont with a thousand horsemen, and, having disarmed the Earl of Huntly, Livingston, and Melville, who had returned to his mistress, he seized the queen's horse by the bridle, and with apparent violence he forced Mary to turn back and follow him to Dunbar; which the queen did without any resistance—a strange thing for one of Mary's character.

The day following, the Earls of Huntly, Livingston, Melville, and the people in their train were set at liberty; then, ten days afterwards, Bothwell and the queen, perfectly reconciled, returned to Edinburgh together.

Two days after this return, Bothwell gave a great dinner to the nobles his partisans in a tavern. When the meal was ended, on the very same table, amid half-drained glasses and empty bottles, Lindsay, Ruthven, Morton, Maitland, and a dozen or fifteen other noblemen signed a bond which not only set forth that upon their souls and consciences Bothwell was innocent, but which further denoted him as the most suitable husband for the queen. This bond concluded with this sufficiently strange declaration:

"After all, the queen cannot do otherwise, since the earl has carried her off and has lain with her."

Yet two circumstances were still opposed to this marriage: the first, that Bothwell had already been married three times, and that his three wives were living; the second, that having carried off the queen, this violence might cause to be regarded as null the alliance which she should contract with him: the first of these objections was attended to, to begin with, as the one most difficult to solve.

Bothwell's two first wives were of obscure birth, consequently he scorned to disquiet himself about them; but it was not so with the third, a daughter of that Earl of Huntly who been trampled beneath the horses' feet, and a sister of Gordon, who had been decapitated. Fortunately for Bothwell, his past behaviour made his wife long for a divorce with an eagerness as great as his own. There was not much difficulty, then, in persuading her to bring a charge of adultery against her husband. Bothwell confessed that he had had criminal intercourse with a relative of his wife, and the Archbishop of St. Andrews, the same who had taken up his abode in that solitary house at Kirk of Field to be present at Darnley's death, pronounced the marriage null. The case was begun, pushed on, and decided in ten days.

As to the second obstacle, that of the violence used to the queen, Mary undertook to remove it herself; for, being brought before the court, she declared that not only did she pardon Bothwell for his conduct as regarded her, but further that, knowing him to be a good and faithful subject, she intended raising him immediately to new honours. In fact, some days afterwards she created him Duke of Orkney, and on the 15th of the same month—that is to say, scarcely four months after the death of Darnley—with levity that resembled madness, Mary, who had petitioned for a dispensation to wed a Catholic prince, her cousin in the third degree, married Bothwell, a Protestant upstart, who, his divorce notwithstanding, was still bigamous, and who thus found himself in the position of having four wives living, including the queen.

The wedding was dismal, as became a festival under such outrageous auspices. Morton, Maitland, and some base flatterers of Bothwell alone were present at it. The French ambassador, although he was a creature of the House of Guise, to which the queen belonged, refused to attend it.

Mary's delusion was short-lived: scarcely was she in Bothwell's power than she saw what a master she had given herself. Gross, unfeeling, and violent, he seemed chosen by Providence to avenge the faults of which he had been the instigator or the accomplice. Soon his fits of passion reached such a point, that one day, no longer able to endure them, Mary seized a dagger from Erskine, who was present with Melville at one of these scenes, and would have struck herself, saying that she would rather die than continue living unhappily as she did; yet, inexplicable as it seems, in spite of these miseries, renewed without ceasing, Mary, forgetting that she was wife and queen, tender and submissive as a child, was always the first to be reconciled with Bothwell.

Nevertheless, these public scenes gave a pretext to the nobles, who only sought an opportunity for an outbreak. The Earl of Mar, the young prince's tutor, Argyll, Athol, Glencairn, Lindley, Boyd, and even Morton and Maitland themselves, those eternal accomplices of Bothwell, rose, they said, to avenge the death of the king, and to draw the son from hands which had killed the father and which were keeping the mother captive. As to Murray, he had kept completely in the background during all the last events; he was in the county of Fife when the king was assassinated, and three days before the trial of Bothwell he had asked and obtained from his sister permission to take a journey on the Continent.

The insurrection took place in such a prompt and instantaneous manner, that the Confederate lords, whose plan was to surprise and seize both Mary and Bothwell, thought they would succeed at the first attempt.

The king and queen were at table with Lord Borthwick, who was entertaining them, when suddenly it was announced that a large body of armed men was surrounding the castle: Bothwell and Mary suspected that they were aimed at, and as they had no means of resistance, Bothwell dressed himself as a squire, Mary as a page, and both immediately taking horse, escaped by one door just as the Confederates were coming in by the other. The fugitives withdrew to Dunbar.

There they called together all Bothwell's friends, and made them sign a kind of treaty by which they undertook to defend the queen and her husband. In the midst of all this, Murray arrived from France, and Bothwell offered the document to him as to the others; but Murray refused to put his signature to it, saying that it was insulting him to think he need be bound by a written agreement when it was a question of defending his sister and his queen. This refusal having led to an altercation between him and Bothwell, Murray, true to his system of neutrality, withdrew into his earldom, and let affairs follow without him the fatal decline they had taken.

In the meantime the Confederates, after having failed at Borthwick, not feeling strong enough to attack Bothwell at Dunbar, marched upon Edinburgh, where they had an understanding with a man of whom Bothwell thought himself sure. This man was James Balfour, governor of the citadel, the same who had presided over the preparation of the mine which had blown up Darnley, and whom Bothwell had, met on entering the garden at Kirk of Field. Not only did Balfour deliver Edinburgh Castle into the hands of the Confederates, but he also gave them a little silver coffer of which the cipher, an "F" crowned, showed that it had belonged to Francis II; and in fact it was a gift from her first husband, which the queen had presented to Bothwell. Balfour stated that this coffer contained precious papers, which in the present circumstances might be of great use to Mary's enemies. The Confederate lords opened it, and found inside the three genuine or spurious letters that we have quoted, the marriage contract of Mary and Bothwell, and twelve poems in the queen's handwriting. As Balfour had said, therein lay, for her enemies, a rich and precious find, which was worth more than a victory; for a victory would yield them only the queen's life, while Balfour's treachery yielded them her honour.

CHAPTER IV

Meanwhile Bothwell had levied some troops, and thought himself in a position to hold the country: accordingly, he set out with his army, without even waiting for the Hamiltons, who were assembling their vassals, and June 15th, 1567, the two opposed forces were face to face. Mary, who desired to try to avoid bloodshed, immediately sent the French ambassador to the Confederate lords to exhort them to lay aside their arms; but they replied "that the queen deceived herself in taking them for rebels; that they were marching not against her, but against Bothwell." Then the king's friends did what they could to break off the negotiations and give battle: it was already too late; the soldiers knew that they were defending the cause of one man, and that they were going to fight for a woman's caprice, and not for the good of the country: they cried aloud, then, that "since Bothwell alone was aimed at, it was for Bothwell to defend his cause". And he, vain and blustering as usual, gave out that he was ready to prove his innocence in person against whomsoever would dare to maintain that he was guilty. Immediately everyone with any claim to nobility in the rival camp accepted the challenge; and as the honour was given to the bravest, Kirkcaldy of Grange, Murray of Tullibardine, and Lord Lindsay of Byres defied him successively. But, be it that courage failed him, be it that in the moment of danger he did not himself believe in the justice of his cause, he, to escape the combat, sought such strange pretexts that the queen herself was ashamed; and his most devoted friends murmured.

Then Mary, perceiving the fatal humour of men's minds, decided not to run the risk of a battle. She sent a herald to Kirkcaldy of Grange, who was commanding an outpost, and as he was advancing without distrust to converse with the queen, Bothwell, enraged at his own cowardice, ordered a soldier to fire upon him; but this time Mary herself interposed, forbidding him under pain of death to offer the least violence. In the meanwhile, as the imprudent order given by Bothwell spread through the army, such murmurs burst forth that he clearly saw that his cause was for ever lost.

That is what the queen thought also; for the result of her conference with Lord Kirkcaldy was that she should abandon Bothwell's cause, and pass over into the camp of the Confederates, on condition that they would lay down their arms before her and bring her as queen to Edinburgh. Kirkcaldy left her to take these conditions to the nobles, and promised to return next day with a satisfactory answer. But at the moment of leaving Bothwell, Mary was seized again with that fatal love for him that she was never able to surmount, and felt herself overcome with such weakness, that, weeping bitterly, and before everyone, she wanted Kirkcaldy to be told that she broke off all negotiations; however, as Bothwell had understood that he was no longer safe in camp, it was he who insisted that things should remain as they were; and, leaving Mary in tears, he mounted, and setting off at full speed, he did not stop till he reached Dunbar.

Next day, at the time appointed, the arrival of Lord

Kirkcaldy of Grange was announced by the trumpeters preceding him. Mary mounted directly and went to meet him; them, as he alighted to greet her, "My lord;" said she, "I surrender to you, on the conditions that you have proposed to me on the part of the nobles, and here is my hand as a sign of entire confidence". Kirkcaldy then knelt down, kissed, the queen's hand respectfully; and, rising, he took her horse by the bridle and led it towards the Confederates' camp.

Everyone of any rank in the army received her with such marks of respect as entirely to satisfy her; but it was not so at all with the soldiers and common people. Hardly had the queen reached the second line, formed by them, than great murmurs arose, and several voices cried, "To the stake, the adulteress! To the stake, the parricide!" However, Mary bore these outrages stoically enough but a more terrible trial yet was in store for her. Suddenly she saw rise before her a banner, on which was depicted on one side the king dead and stretched out in the fatal garden, and on the other the young prince kneeling, his hands joined and his eyes raised to heaven, with this inscription, "O Lord! judge and revenge my cause!" Mary reined in her horse abruptly at this sight, and wanted to turn back; but she had scarcely moved a few paces when the accusing banner again blocked her passage. Wherever she went, she met this dreadful apparition. For two hours she had incessantly under her eyes the king's corpse asking vengeance, and the young prince her son praying God to punish the murderers. At last she could endure it no longer, and, crying out, she threw herself back, having completely lost consciousness, and would have fallen, if someone had not caught hold of her. In the evening she entered Edinburgh, always preceded by the cruel banner, and she already had rather the air of a prisoner than of a queen; for, not having had a moment during the day to attend to her toilet, her hair was falling in disorder about her shoulders, her face was pale and showed traces of tears; and finally, her clothes were covered with dust and mud. As she proceeded through the town, the hootings of the people and the curses of the crowd followed her. At last, half dead with fatigue, worn out with grief, bowed down with shame, she reached the house of the Lord Provost; but scarcely had she got there when the entire population of Edinburgh crowded into the square, with cries that from time to time assumed a tone of terrifying menace. Several times, then, Mary wished to go to the window, hoping that the sight of her, of which she had so often proved the influence, would disarm this multitude; but each time she saw this banner unfurling itself like a bloody curtain between herself and the people—a terrible rendering of their feelings.

However, all this hatred was meant still more for Bothwell than for her: they were pursuing Bothwell in Darnley's widow. The curses were for Bothwell: Bothwell was the adulterer, Bothwell was the murderer, Bothwell was the coward; while Mary was the weak, fascinated woman, who, that same evening, gave afresh proof of her folly.

In fact, directly the falling night had scattered the crowd and a little quiet was regained, Mary, ceasing to be uneasy on her own account, turned immediately to Bothwell, whom she had been obliged to abandon, and who was now proscribed and fleeing; while she, as she believed, was about to reassume her title and station of queen. With that eternal confidence of the woman in her own love, by which she invariably measures the love of another, she thought that Bothwell's greatest distress was to have lost, not wealth and power, but to have lost herself. So she wrote him a long letter, in which, forgetful of herself, she promised him with the most tender expressions of love never to desert him, and to recall him to her directly the breaking up of the Confederate lords should give her power to do so; then, this letter written, she called a soldier, gave him a purse of gold, and charged him to take this letter to Dunbar, where Bothwell ought to be, and if he were already gone, to follow him until he came up with him.

Then she went to bed and slept more calmly; for, unhappy as she was, she believed she had just sweetened misfortunes still greater than hers.

Next day the queen was awakened by the step of an armed man who entered her room. Both astonished and frightened at this neglect of propriety, which could augur nothing good, Mary sat up in bed, and parting the curtains, saw standing before her Lord Lindsay of Byres: she knew he was one of her oldest friends, so she asked him in a voice which she vainly tried to make confident, what he wanted of her at such a time.

"Do you know this writing, madam?" Lord Lindsay asked in a rough voice, presenting to the queen the letter she had written to Bothwell at night, which the soldier had carried to the Confederate lords, instead of taking to its address.

"Yes, doubtless, my lord," the queen answered; "but am I already a prisoner, then, that my correspondence is intercepted? or is it no longer allowed to a wife to write to her husband?"

"When the husband is a traitor," replied Lindsay, "no, madam, it is no longer allowed to a wife to write to her husband—at least, however, if this wife have a part in his treason; which seems to me, besides, quite proved by the promise you make to this wretch to recall him to you."

"My lord," cried Mary, interrupting Lindsay, "do you forget that you are speaking to your queen?"

"There was a time, madam," Lindsay replied, "when I should have spoken to you in a more gentle voice, and bending the knee, although it is not in the nature of us old Scotch to model ourselves on your French courtiers; but for some time, thanks to your changing loves, you have kept us so often in the field, in harness, that our voices are hoarse from the cold night air, and our stiff knees can no longer bend in our armour: you must then take me just as I am, madam; since to-day, for the welfare of Scotland, you are no longer at liberty to choose your favourites."

Mary grew frightfully pale at this want of respect, to which she was not yet accustomed; but quickly containing her anger, as far as possible—

"But still, my lord," said she, "however disposed I may be to take you as you are, I must at least know by what right you come here. That letter which you are holding in your hand would lead me to think it is as a spy, if the ease with which you enter my room without being asked did not make me believe it is as a gaoler. Have the goodness, then, to inform me by which of these two names I must call you."

"Neither by one nor the other, madam; for I am simply your fellow-traveller, chef of the escort which is to take you to Lochleven Castle, your future residence. And yet, scarcely have I arrived there than I shall be obliged to leave you to go and assist the Confederate lords choose a regent for the kingdom."

"So," said Mary, "it was as prisoner and not as queen that I surrendered to Lord Kirkcaldy. It seems to me that things were agreed upon otherwise; but I am glad to see how much time Scotch noblemen need to betray their sworn undertakings".

"Your Grace forgets that these engagements were made on one condition," Lindsay answered.

"On which?" Mary asked.

"That you should separate for ever from your husband's murderer; and there is the proof," he added, showing the letter, "that you had forgotten your promise before we thought of revoking ours."

"And at what o'clock is my departure fixed?" said Mary, whom this discussion was beginning to fatigue.

"At eleven o'clock, madam."

"It is well, my lord; as I have no desire to make your lordship wait, you will have the goodness, in withdrawing, to send me someone to help me dress, unless I am reduced to wait upon myself."

And, in pronouncing these words, Mary made a gesture so imperious, that whatever may have been Lindsay's wish to reply, he bowed and went out. Behind him entered Mary Seyton.

CHAPTER V

At the time appointed the queen was ready: she had suffered so much at Edinburgh that she left it without any regret. Besides, whether to spare her the humiliations of the day before, or to conceal her departure from any partisans who might remain to her, a litter had been made ready. Mary got into it without any resistance, and after two hours' journey she reached Duddington; there a little vessel was waiting for her, which set sail directly she was on board, and next day at dawn she disembarked on the other side of the Firth of Forth in the county of Fife.

Mary halted at Rosythe Castle only just long enough to breakfast, and immediately recommenced her journey; for Lord Lindsay had declared that he wished to reach his destination that same evening. Indeed, as the sun was setting, Mary perceived gilded with his last rays the high towers of Lochleven Castle, situated on an islet in the midst of the lake of the same name.

No doubt the royal prisoner was already expected at Lochleven Castle, for, on reaching the lake side, Lord Lindsay's equerry unfurled his banner, which till then had remained in its case, and waved it from right to left, while his master blew a little hunting bugle which he wore hanging from his neck. A boat immediately put off from the island and came towards the arrivals, set in motion by four vigorous oarsmen, who had soon propelled it across the space which separated it from the bank. Mary silently got into it, and sat down at the stern, while Lord Lindsay and his equerry stood up before her; and as her guide did not seem any more inclined to speak than she was herself to respond, she had plenty of time to examine her future dwelling.

The castle, or rather the fortress of Lochleven, already somewhat gloomy in its situation and architecture, borrowed fresh mournfulness still from the hour at which it appeared to the queen's gaze. It was, so far as she could judge amid the mists rising from the lake, one of those massive structures of the twelfth century which seem, so fast shut up are they, the stone armour of a giant. As she drew near, Mary began to make out the contours of two great round towers, which flanked the corners and gave it the severe character of a state prison. A clump of ancient trees enclosed by a high wall, or rather by a rampart, rose at its north front, and seemed vegetation in stone, and completed the general effect of this gloomy abode, while, on the contrary, the eye wandering from it and passing from islands to islands, lost itself in the west, in the north, and in the south, in the vast plain of Kinross, or stopped southwards at the jagged summits of Ben Lomond, whose farthest slopes died down on the shores of the lake.

Three persons awaited Mary at the castle door: Lady Douglas, William Douglas her son, and a child of twelve who was called Little Douglas, and who was neither a son nor a brother of the inhabitants of the castle, but merely a distant relative. As one can imagine, there were few compliments between Mary and her hosts; and the queen, conducted to her apartment, which was on the first floor, and of which the windows overlooked the lake, was soon left with Mary Seyton, the only one of the four Marys who had been allowed to accompany her.

However, rapid as the interview had been, and short and measured the words exchanged between the prisoner and her gaolers, Mary had had time, together with what she knew of them beforehand, to construct for herself a fairly accurate idea of the new personages who had just mingled in her history.

Lady Lochleven, wife of Lord William Douglas, of whom we have already said a few words at the beginning of this history, was a woman of from fifty-five to sixty years of age, who had been handsome enough in her youth to fix upon herself the glances of King James V, and who had had a son by him, who was this same Murray whom we have already seen figuring so often in Mary's history, and who, although his birth was illegitimate, had always been treated as a brother by the queen.

Lady Lochleven had had a momentary hope, so great was the king's love for her, of becoming his wife, which upon the whole was possible, the family of Mar, from which she was descended, being the equal of the most ancient and the noblest families in Scotland. But, unluckily, perhaps slanderously, certain talk which was circulating among the young noblemen of the time came to James's ears; it was said that together with her royal lover the beautiful favourite had another, whom she had chosen, no doubt from curiosity, from the very lowest class. It was added that this Porterfield, or

Porterfield, was the real father of the child who had already received the name of James Stuart, and whom the king was educating as his son at the monastery of St. Andrews. These rumours, well founded or not, had therefore stopped James V at the moment when, in gratitude to her who had given him a son, he was on the point of raising her to the rank of queen; so that, instead of marrying her himself, he had invited her to choose among the nobles at court; and as she was very handsome, and the king's favour went with the marriage, this choice, which fell on Lord William Douglas of Lochleven, did not meet with any resistance on his part. However, in spite of this direct protection, that James V preserved for her all his life, Lady Douglas could never forget that she had fingered higher fortune; moreover, she had a hatred for the one who, according to herself, had usurped her place, and poor Mary had naturally inherited the profound animosity that Lady Douglas bore to her mother, which had already come to light in the few words that the two women had exchanged. Besides, in ageing, whether from repentance for her errors or from hypocrisy, Lady Douglas had become a prude and a puritan; so that at this time she united with the natural acrimony of her character all the stiffness of the new religion she had adopted.

William Douglas, who was the eldest son of Lord Lochleven, on his mother's side half-brother of Murray, was a man of from thirty-five to thirty-six years of age, athletic, with hard and strongly pronounced features, red-haired like all the younger branch, and who had inherited that paternal hatred that for a century the Douglases cherished against the Stuarts, and which was shown by so many plots, rebellions, and assassinations. According as fortune had favoured or deserted Murray, William Douglas had seen the rays of the fraternal star draw near or away from him; he had then felt that he was living in another's life, and was devoted, body and soul, to him who was his cause of greatness or of abasement. Mary's fall, which must necessarily raise Murray, was thus a source of joy for him, and the Confederate lords could not have chosen better than in confiding the safe-keeping of their prisoner to the instinctive spite of Lady Douglas and to the intelligent hatred of her son.

As to Little Douglas, he was, as we have said, a child of twelve, for some months an orphan, whom the Lochlevens had taken charge of, and whom they made buy the bread they gave him by all sorts of harshness. The result was that the child, proud and spiteful as a Douglas, and knowing, although his fortune was inferior, that his birth was equal to his proud relatives, had little by little changed his early gratitude into lasting and profound hatred: for one used to say that among the Douglases there was an age for loving, but that there was none for hating. It results that, feeling his weakness and isolation, the child was self-contained with strength beyond his years, and, humble and submissive in appearance, only awaited the moment when, a grown-up young man, he could leave Lochleven, and perhaps avenge himself for the proud protection of those who dwelt there. But the feelings that we have just expressed did not extend to all the members of the family: as much as from the bottom of his heart the little Douglas detested William and his mother, so much he loved George, the second of Lady Lochleven's sons, of whom we have not yet spoken, because, being away from the castle when the queen arrived, we have not yet found an opportunity to present him to our readers.

George, who at this time might have been about twenty-five or twenty-six years old, was the second son of Lord Lochleven; but by a singular chance, that his mother's adventurous youth had caused Sir William to interpret amiss, this second son had none of the characteristic features of the Douglases' full cheeks, high colour, large ears, and red hair. The result was that poor George, who, on the contrary, had been given by nature pale cheeks, dark blue eyes, and black hair, had been since coming into the world an object of indifference to his father and of dislike to his elder brother. As to his mother, whether she were indeed in good faith surprised like Lord Douglas at this difference in race, whether she knew the cause and inwardly reproached herself, George had never been, ostensibly at least, the object of a very lively maternal affection; so the young man, followed from his childhood by a fatality that he could not explain, had sprung up like a wild shrub, full of sap and strength, but uncultivated and solitary. Besides, from the time when he was fifteen, one was accustomed to his motiveless absences, which the indifference that everyone bore him made moreover perfectly explicable; from time to time, however, he was seen to reappear at the castle, like those migratory birds which always return to the same place but only stay a moment, then take their way again without one's knowing towards what spot in the world they are directing their flight.

An instinct of misfortune in common had drawn Little Douglas to George. George, seeing the child ill-treated by everyone, had conceived an affection for him, and Little Douglas, feeling himself loved amid the atmosphere of indifference around him, turned with open arms and heart to George: it resulted from this mutual liking that one day, when the child had committed I do not know what fault, and that William Douglas raised the whip he beat his dogs with to strike him, that George, who was sitting on a stone, sad and thoughtful, had immediately sprung up, snatched the whip from his brother's hands and had thrown it far from him. At this insult William had drawn his sword, and George his, so that these two brothers, who had hated one another for twenty years like two enemies, were going to cut one another's throats, when Little Douglas, who had picked up the whip, coming back and kneeling before William, offered him the ignominious weapon, saying,

"Strike, cousin; I have deserved it."

This behaviour of the child had caused some minutes' reflection to the two young men, who, terrified at the crime they were about to commit, had returned their swords to their scabbards and had each gone away in silence. Since this incident the friendship of George and Little Douglas had acquired new strength, and on the child's side it had become veneration.

We dwell upon all these details somewhat at length, perhaps, but no doubt our readers will pardon us when they see the use to be made of them.

This is the family, less George, who, as we have said, was absent at the time of her arrival, into the midst of which the queen had fallen, passing in a moment from the summit of power to the position of a prisoner; for from the day following her arrival Mary saw that it was by such a title she was an inmate of Lochleven Castle. In fact, Lady Douglas presented herself before her as soon as it was morning, and with an embarrassment and dislike ill disguised beneath an appearance of respectful indifference, invited Mary to follow her and take stock of the several parts of the fortress which had been chosen beforehand for her private use. She then made her go through three rooms, of which one was to serve as her bedroom, the second as sitting-room, and the third as ante-chamber; afterwards, leading the way down a spiral staircase, which looked into the great hall of the castle, its only outlet, she had crossed this hall, and had taken Mary into the garden whose trees the queen had seen topping the high walls on her arrival: it was a little square of ground, forming a flower-bed in the midst of which was an artificial fountain. It was entered by a very low door, repeated in the opposite wall; this second door looked on to the lake and, like all the castle doors, whose keys, however, never left the belt or the pillow of William Douglas, it was guarded night and day by a sentinel. This was now the whole domain of her who had possessed the palaces, the plains, and the mountains of an entire kingdom.

Mary, on returning to her room, found breakfast ready, and William Douglas standing near the table he was going to fulfil about the queen the duties of carver and taster.

In spite of their hatred for Mary, the Douglases would have considered it an eternal blemish on their honour if any accident should have befallen the queen while she was dwelling in their castle; and it was in order that the queen herself should not entertain any fear in this respect that William Douglas, in his quality of lord of the manor, had not only desired to carve before the queen, but even to taste first in her presence, all the dishes served to her, as well as the water and the several wines to be brought her. This precaution saddened Mary more than it reassured her; for she understood that, while she stayed in the castle, this ceremony would prevent any intimacy at table. However, it proceeded from too noble an intention for her to impute it as a crime to her hosts: she resigned herself, then, to this company, insupportable as it was to her; only, from that day forward, she so cut short her meals that all the time she was at Lochleven her longest dinners barely lasted more than a quarter of an hour.

Two days after her arrival, Mary, on sitting down to table for breakfast, found on her plate a letter addressed to her which had been put there by William Douglas. Mary recognised Murray's handwriting, and her first feeling was one of joy; for if a ray of hope remained to her, it came from her brother, to whom she had always been perfectly kind, whom from Prior of St. Andrew's she had made an earl in bestowing on him the splendid estates which formed part of the old earldom of Murray, and to whom, which was of more importance, she had since pardoned, or pretended to pardon, the part he had taken in Rizzio's assassination.

Her astonishment was great, then, when, having opened the letter, she found in it bitter reproaches for her conduct, an exhortation to do penance, and an assurance several times repeated that she should never leave her prison. He ended his letter in announcing to her that, in spite of his distaste for public affairs, he had been obliged to accept the regency, which he had done less for his country than for his sister, seeing that it was the sole means he had of standing in the way of the ignominious trial to which the nobles wished to bring her, as author, or at least as chief accomplice, of Darnley's death. This imprisonment was then clearly a great good fortune for her, and she ought to thank Heaven for it, as an alleviation of the fate awaiting her if he had not interceded for her.

This letter was a lightning stroke for Mary: only, as she did not wish to give her enemies the delight of seeing her suffer, she contained her grief, and, turning to William Douglas—

"My lord," said she, "this letter contains news that you doubtless know already, for although we are not children by the same mother, he who writes to me is related to us in the same degree, and will not have desired to write to his sister without writing to his brother at the same time; besides, as a good son, he will have desired to acquaint his mother with the unlooked-for greatness that has befallen him."

"Yes, madam," replied William, "we know since yesterday that, for the welfare of Scotland, my brother has been named regent; and as he is a son as respectful to his mother as he is devoted to his country, we hope that he will repair the evil that for five years favourites of every sort and kind have done to both."

"It is like a good son, and at the same time like a courteous host, to go back no farther into the history of Scotland," replied Mary Stuart, "and not to make the daughter blush for the father's errors; for I have heard say that the evil which your lordship laments was prior to the time to which you assign it, and that King James V. also had formerly favourites, both male and female. It is true that they add that the ones as ill rewarded his friendship as the others his love. In this, if you are ignorant of it, my lord, you can be instructed, if he is still living, by a certain. Porterfeld or Porterfield, I don't know which, understanding these names of the lower classes too ill to retain and pronounce them, but about which, in my stead, your noble mother could give you information."

With these words, Mary Stuart rose, and, leaving William Douglas crimson with rage, she returned into her bedroom, and bolted the door behind her.

All that day Mary did not come down, remaining at her window, from which she at least enjoyed a splendid view over the plains and village of Kinross; but this vast extent only contracted her heart the more, when, bringing her gaze back from the horizon to the castle, she beheld its walls surrounded on all sides by the deep waters of the lake, on whose wide surface a single boat, where Little Douglas was fishing, was rocking like a speck. For some moments Mary's eyes mechanically rested on this child, whom she had already seen upon her arrival, when suddenly a horn sounded from the Kinross side. At the same moment Little Douglas threw away his line, and began to row towards the shore whence the signal had come with skill and strength beyond his years. Mary, who had let her gaze rest on him absently, continued to follow him with her eyes, and saw him make for a spot on the shore so distant that the boat seemed to her at length but an imperceptible speck; but soon it reappeared, growing larger as it approached, and Mary could then observe that it was bringing back to the castle a new passenger, who, having in his turn taken the oars, made the little skiff fly over the tranquil water of the lake, where it left a furrow gleaming in the last rays of the sun. Very soon, flying on with the swiftness of a bird, it was near enough for Mary to see that the skilful and vigorous oarsman was a young man from twenty-five to twenty-six years of age, with long black hair, clad in a close coat of green cloth, and wearing a Highlander's cap, adorned with an eagle's feather; then, as with his back turned to the window he drew nearer, Little Douglas, who was leaning on his shoulder, said a few words which made him turn round towards the queen: immediately Mary, with an instinctive movement rather than with the dread of being an object of idle curiosity, drew back, but not so quickly, however, but that she had been able to see the handsome pale face of the unknown, who, when she returned to the window, had disappeared behind one of the corners of the castle.

Everything is a cause of conjecture to a prisoner: it seemed to Mary that this young man's face was not unknown to her, and that he had seen her already; but though great the care with which she questioned her memory, she could not recall any distinct remembrance, so much so that the queen ended in thinking it the play of her imagination, or that some vague and distinct resemblance had deceived her.

However, in spite of Mary, this idea had taken an important place in her mind: she incessantly saw this little boat skimming the water, and the young man and the child who were in it drawing near her, as if to bring her help. It followed that, although there had been nothing real in all these captive's dreams, she slept that night a calmer sleep than she had yet done since she had been in Lochleven Castle.

Next day, on rising, Mary ran to her window: the weather was fine, and everything seemed to smile on her, the water, the heavens and the earth. But, without being able to account for the restraining motive, she did not want to go down into the ga den before breakfast. When the door opened, 'she turned quickly round: it was, as on the day before, William Douglas, who came to fulfil his duty as taster.

The breakfast was a short and silent one; then, as soon as Douglas had withdrawn, Mary descended in her turn: in crossing the courtyard she saw two horses ready saddled, which pointed to the near departure of a master and a squire. Was it the young man with the black hair already setting out again? This is what Mary did not dare or did not wish to ask. She consequently went her way, and entered the garden: at the first glance she took it in in its full extent; it was deserted.

Mary walked there a moment; then, soon tiring of the promenade, she went up again to her room: in passing back through the courtyard she had noticed that the horses were no longer there. Directly she returned into her apartment, she went then to the window to see if she could discover anything upon the lake to guide her in her conjectures: a boat was in fact receding, and in this boat were the two horses and the two horsemen; one was William Douglas, the other a simple squire from the house.

Mary continued watching the boat until it had touched the shore. Arrived there, the two horsemen got out, disembarked their horses, and went away at full gallop, taking the same road by which the queen had come; so that, as the horses were prepared for a long journey, Mary thought that William Douglas was going to Edinburgh. As to the boat, scarcely had it landed its two passengers on the opposite shore than it returned towards the castle.

At that moment Mary Seyton announced to the queen that Lady Douglas was asking permission to visit her.

It was the second time, after long hatred on Lady Douglas's part and contemptuous indifference on the queen's, that the two women were face to face; therefore the queen, with that instinctive impulse of coquetry which urges women, in whatever situation they find themselves, to desire to be beautiful, above all for women, made a sign to Mary Seyton, and, going to a little mirror fastened to the wall in a heavy Gothic frame, she arranged her curls, and readjusted the lace of her collar; then; having seated herself in the pose most favourable to her, in a great arm-chair, the only one in her sitting-room, she said smilingly to Mary Seyton that she might admit Lady Douglas, who was immediately introduced.

Mary's expectation was not disappointed: Lady Douglas, in spite of her hatred for James Vs daughter, and mistress of herself as she thought she as, could not prevent herself from showing by a movement of surprise the impression that this marvelous beauty was making on her: she thought she should find Mary crushed by her unhappiness, pallid from her fatigues, humbled by captivity, and she saw hers calm, lovely, and haughty as usual. Mary perceived the effect that she was producing, and addressing herself with an ironical smile partly to Mary Seyton, who was leaning on the back of her chair, and partly to her who was paying her this unforeseen visit.

"We are fortunate to-day," said she, "for we are going as it seems to enjoy the society of our good hostess, whom we thank besides for having kindly maintained with us the empty ceremony of announcing herself—a ceremony with which, having the keys of our apartment, she could have dispensed."

"If my presence is inconvenient to your grace," replied Lady

Lochleven, "I am all the more sorry for it, as circumstances will oblige me to impose it twice daily, at least during the absence of my son, who is summoned to Edinburgh by the regent; this is of what I came to inform your grace, not with the empty ceremonial of the court, but with the consideration which Lady Lochleven owes to everyone who has received hospitality in her castle."

"Our good hostess mistakes our intention," Mary answered, with affected good-nature; "and the regent himself can bear witness to the pleasure we have always had in bringing nearer to us the persons who can recall to us, even indirectly, our well-beloved father, James V. It will be therefore unjustly that Lady Douglas will interpret in a manner disagreeable to herself our surprise at seeing her; and the hospitality that she offers us so obligingly does not promise us, in spite of her goodwill, sufficient distractions that we should deprive ourselves of those that her visits cannot fail to procure us."

"Unfortunately, madam," replied Lady Lochleven, whom Mary was keeping standing before her, "whatever pleasure I myself derive from these visits, I shall be obliged to deprive myself of, except at the times I have mentioned. I am now too old to bear fatigue, and I have, always been too proud to endure sarcasms."

"Really, Seyton," cried Mary, seeming to recollect herself, "we had not dreamed that Lady Lochleven, having won her right to a stool at the court of the king my father, would have need to preserve it in the prison of the queen his daughter. Bring forward a seat, Seyton, that we be not deprived so soon, and by a failure of memory on our part, of our gracious hostess's company; or even," went on Mary, rising and pointing out her own seat to Lady Lochleven, who was making a motion to withdraw, "if a stool does not suit you, my lady, take this easy-chair: you will not be the first member of your family to sit in my place."

At this last allusion, which recalled to her Murray's usurpation, Lady Lochleven was no doubt about to make some exceedingly bitter reply, when the young man with the dark hair appeared on the threshold, without being announced, and, advancing towards Lady Lochleven, without saluting Mary—

"Madam," said he, bowing to the former, "the boat which took my brother has just returned, and one of the men in it is charged with a pressing charge that Lord William forgot to make to you himself."

Then, saluting the old lady with the same respect, he immediately went out of the room, without even glancing at the queen, who, hurt by this impertinence, turned round to Mary Seyton, and, with her usual calm—

"What have they told us, Seyton, of injurious rumours which were spread about our worthy hostess apropos of a child with a pale face and dark hair? If this child, as I have every reason to believe, has become the young man who just went out of the room, I am ready to affirm to all the incredulous that he is a true Douglas, if not for courage, of which we cannot judge, then for insolence, of which he has just given us proofs. Let us return, darling," continued the queen, leaning on Mary Seyton's arm; "for our good hostess, out of courtesy, might think herself obliged to keep us company longer, while we know that she is impatiently awaited elsewhere."

With these words, Mary went into her bedroom; while the old lady, still quite stunned with the shower of sarcasms that the queen had rained on her, withdrew, murmuring, "Yes, yes, he is a Douglas, and with God's help he will prove it, I hope."

The queen had had strength as long as she was sustained by her enemy's presence, but scarcely was she alone than she sank into a chair, and no longer having any witness of her weakness than Mary Seyton, burst into tears. Indeed, she had just been cruelly wounded: till then no man had come near her who had not paid homage either to the majesty of her rank or to the beauty of her countenance. But precisely he, on whom she had reckoned, without knowing why, with instinctive hopes, insulted her at one and the same time in her double pride of queen and woman: thus she remained shut up till evening.

At dinner-time, just as Lady Lochleven had informed Mary, she ascended to the queen's apartment, in her dress of honour, and preceding four servants who were carrying the several dishes composing the prisoner's repast, and who, in their turn, were followed by the old castle steward, having, as on days of great ceremony, his gold chain round his neck and his ivory stick in his hand. The servants' placed the dishes on the table, and waited in silence for the moment when it should please the queen to come out of her room; but at this moment the door opened, and in place of the queen Mary Seyton appeared.

"Madam," said she on entering, "her grace was indisposed during the day, and will take nothing this evening; it will be useless, then, for you to wait longer."

"Permit me to hope," replied Lady Lochleven, "that she will change her decision; in any case, see me perform my office."

At these words, a servant handed Lady Lochleven bread and salt on a silver salver, while the old steward, who, in the absence of William Douglas, fulfilled the duties of carver, served to her on a plate of the same metal a morsel from each of the dishes that had been brought; then, this transaction ended.

"So the queen will not appear to-day?" Lady Lochleven inquired.

"It is her Majesty's resolve," replied Mary Seyton.

"Our presence is then needless," said the old lady; "but in any case the table is served, and if her grace should have need of anything else, she would have but to name it."

With these words, Lady Lochleven, with the same stiffness and the same dignity with which she had come, withdrew, followed by her four servants and her steward.

As Lady Lochleven had foreseen, the queen, yielding to the entreaties of Mary Seyton, came out of her room at last, towards eight o'clock in the evening, sat down to table, and, served by the only maid of honour left her, ate a little; then, getting up, she went to the window.

It was one of those magnificent summer evenings on which the whole of nature seems making holiday: the sky was studded with stars, which were reflected in the lake, and in their midst, like a more fiery star, the flame of the chafing-dish shone, burning at the stern of a little boat: the queen, by the gleam of the light it shed, perceived George Douglas and Little Douglas, who were fishing. However great her wish to profit by this fine evening to breathe the pure night air, the sight of this young man who had so grossly insulted her this very day made such a keen impression on her that she shut her window directly, and, retiring into her room, went to bed, and made her companion in captivity read several prayers aloud; then, not being able to sleep, so greatly was she agitated, she rose, and throwing on a mantle went again to the window the boat had disappeared.

Mary spent part of the night gazing into the immensity of the heavens, or into the depths of the lake; but in spite of the nature of the thoughts agitating her, she none the less found very great physical alleviation in contact with this pure air and in contemplation of this peaceful and silent night: thus she awoke next day calmer and more resigned. Unfortunately, the sight of Lady Lochleven, who presented herself at breakfast-time, to fulfil her duties as taster, brought back her irritability. Perhaps, however, things would have gone on smoothly if Lady Lochleven, instead of remaining standing by the sideboard, had withdrawn after having tasted the various dishes of the courses; but this insisting on remaining throughout the meal, which was at bottom a mark of respect, seemed to the queen unbearable tyranny.

"Darling," said she, speaking to Mary Seyton, "have you already forgotten that our good hostess complained yesterday of the fatigue she felt inn standing? Bring her, then, one of the two stools which compose our royal furniture, and take care that it is not the one with the leg broken". "If the furniture of Lochleven Castle is in such bad condition, madam," the old lady replied, "it is the fault of the kings of Scotland: the poor Douglases for nearly a century have had such a small part of their sovereigns' favour, that they have not been able to keep up the splendour of their ancestors to the level of that of private individuals, and because there was in Scotland a certain musician, as I am informed, who spent their income for a whole year in one month."

"Those who know how to take so well, my lady," the queen answered, "have no need of being given to: it seems to me the Douglases have lost nothing by waiting, and there is not a younger son of this noble family who might not aspire to the highest alliances; it is truly vexatious that our sister the queen of England has taken a vow of virginity; as is stated."

"Or rather," interrupted Lady Lochleven, "that the Queen of Scotland is not a widow by her third husband. But," continued the old lady, pretending to recollect herself, "I do not say that to reproach your grace. Catholics look upon marriage as a sacrament, and on this head receive it as often as they can."

"This, then," returned Mary, "is the difference between

them and the Huguenots; for they, not having the same respect for it, think it is allowed them to dispense with it in certain circumstances."

At this terrible sarcasm Lady Lochleven took a step towards Mary Stuart, holding in her hand the knife which she had just been using to cut off a piece of meat brought her to taste; but the queen rose up with so great a calm and with such majesty, that either from involuntary respect or shame of her first impulse, she let fall the weapon she was holding, and not finding anything sufficiently strong in reply to express her feelings, she signed to the servants to follow her, and went out of the apartment with all the dignity that anger permitted her to summon to her aid.

Scarcely had Lady Lochleven left the room than the queen sat down again, joyful and triumphant at the victory she had just gained, and ate with a better appetite than she had yet done since she was a prisoner, while Mary Seyton deplored in a low tone and with all possible respect this fatal gift of repartee that Mary had received, and which, with her beauty, was one of the causes of all her misfortunes; but the queen did nothing but laugh at all her observations, saying she was curious to see the figure her good hostess would cut at dinnertime.

After breakfast, the queen went down into the garden: her satisfied pride had restored some of her cheerfulness, so much so that, seeing, while crossing the hall, a mandolin lying forgotten on a chair, she told Mary Seyton to take it, to see, she said, if she could recall her old talent. In reality the queen was one of the best musicians of the time, and played admirably, says Brantome, on the lute and viol d'amour, an instrument much resembling the mandolin.

Mary Seyton obeyed.

Arrived in the garden, the queen sat down in the deepest shade, and there, having tuned her instrument, she at first drew from it lively and light tones, which soon darkened little by little, at the same time that her countenance assumed a hue of deep melancholy. Mary Seyton looked at her with uneasiness, although for a long time she had been used to these sudden changes in her mistress's humour, and she was about to ask the reason of this gloomy veil suddenly spread over her face, when, regulating her harmonies, Mary began to sing in a low voice, and as if for herself alone, the following verses:

"Caverns, meadows, plains and mounts,
 Lands of tree and stone,
 Rivers, rivulets and founts,
 By which I stray alone,
 Bewailing as I go,
 With tears that overflow,
 Sing will I
 The miserable woe
 That bids me grieve and sigh.

 Ay, but what is here to lend
 Ear to my lament?
 What is here can comprehend

Mary Stuart

My dull discontent?
Neither grass nor reed,
Nor the ripples heed,
Flowing by,
While the stream with speed
Hastens from my eye.

Vainly does my wounded heart
Hope, alas, to heal;
Seeking, to allay its smart,
Things that cannot feel.
Better should my pain
Bitterly complain,
Crying shrill,
To thee who dost constrain
My spirit to such ill.

Goddess, who shalt never die,
List to what I say;
Thou who makest me to lie
Weak beneath thy sway,
If my life must know
Ending at thy blow,
Cruellest!
Own it perished so
But at thy behest.

Lo! my face may all men see

Slowly pine and fade,
E'en as ice doth melt and flee
Near a furnace laid.
Yet the burning ray
Wasting me away
Passion's glow,
Wakens no display
Of pity for my woe.

Yet does every neighbour tree,
Every rocky wall,
This my sorrow know and see;
So, in brief, doth all
Nature know aright
This my sorry plight;
Thou alone
Takest thy delight
To hear me cry and moan.

But if it be thy will,
To see tormented still
Wretched me,
Then let my woful ill
Immortal be."

 This last verse died away as if the queen were exhausted, and at the same time the mandolin slipped from her hands, and would have fallen to the ground had not Mary Seyton thrown herself on her knees and prevented it. The young girl remained thus at her mistress's feet for some time, gazing at her silently, and as she saw that she was losing herself more and more in gloomy reverie—

"Have those lines brought back to your Majesty some sad remembrance?" she asked hesitatingly.

"Oh, yes," answered the queen; "they reminded me of the unfortunate being who composed them."

"And may I, without indiscretion, inquire of your grace who is their author?"

"Alas! he was a noble, brave, and handsome young man, with a faithful heart and a hot head, who would defend me to-day, if I had defended him then; but his boldness seemed to me rashness, and his fault a crime. What was to be done? I did not love him. Poor Chatelard! I was very cruel to him."

"But you did not prosecute him, it was your brother; you did not condemn him, the judges did."

"Yes, yes; I know that he too was Murray's victim, and that is no doubt the reason that I am calling him to mind just now. But I was able to pardon him, Mary, and I was inflexible; I let ascend the scaffold a man whose only crime was in loving me too well; and now I am astonished and complain of being abandoned by everyone. Listen, darling, there is one thing that terrifies me: it is, that when I search within myself I find that I have not only deserved my fate, but even that God did not punish me severely enough."

"What strange thoughts for your grace!" cried Mary; "and see where those unlucky lines which returned to your mind have led you, the very day when you were beginning to recover a little of your cheerfulness."

"Alas!" replied the queen, shaking her head and uttering a deep sigh, "for six years very few days have passed that I have not repeated those lines to myself, although it may be for the first time to-day that I repeat them aloud. He was a Frenchman too, Mary: they have exiled from me, taken or killed all who came to me from France. Do you remember that vessel which was swallowed up before our eyes when we came out of Calais harbour? I exclaimed then that it was a sad omen: you all wanted to reassure me. Well, who was right, now, you or I?"

The queen was in one of those fits of sadness for which tears are the sole remedy; so Mary Seyton, perceiving that not only would every consolation be vain, but also unreasonable, far from continuing to react against her mistress's melancholy, fully agreed with her: it followed that the queen, who was suffocating, began to weep, and that her tears brought her comfort; then little by little she regained self-control, and this crisis passed as usual, leaving her firmer and more resolute than ever, so that when she went up to her room again it was impossible to read the slightest alteration in her countenance.

The dinner-hour was approaching, and Mary, who in the morning was looking forward impatiently to the enjoyment of her triumph over Lady Lochleven, now saw her advance with uneasiness: the mere idea of again facing this woman, whose pride one was always obliged to oppose with insolence, was, after the moral fatigues of the day, a fresh weariness. So she decided not to appear for dinner, as on the day before: she was all the more glad she had taken this resolution, that this time it was not Lady Lochleven who came to fulfil the duties enjoined on a member of the family to make the queen easy, but George Douglas, whom his mother in her displeasure at the morning scene sent to replace her. Thus, when Mary Seyton told the queen that she saw the young man with dark hair cross the courtyard on his way to her, Mary still further congratulated herself on her decision; for this young man's insolence had wounded her more deeply than all his mother's haughty insults. The queen was not a little astonished, then, when in a few minutes Mary Seyton returned and informed her that George Douglas, having sent away the servants, desired the honour of speaking to her on a matter of importance. At first the queen refused; but Mary Seyton told her that the young man's air and manner this time were so different from what she had seen two days before, that she thought her mistress would be wrong to refuse his request.

The queen rose then, and with the pride and majesty habitual to her, entered the adjoining room, and, having taken three steps, stopped with a disdainful air, waiting for George to address her.

Mary Seyton had spoken truly: George Douglas was now another man. To-day he seemed to be as respectful and timid as the preceding day he had seemed haughty and proud. He, in his turn, made a step towards the queen; but seeing Mary Seyton standing behind her—

"Madam," said he, "I wished to speak with your Majesty alone: shall I not obtain this favour?"

"Mary Seyton is not a stranger to me, Sir: she is my sister, my friend; she is more than all that, she is my companion in captivity."

"And by all these claims, madam, I have the utmost veneration for her; but what I have to tell you cannot be heard by other ears than yours. Thus, madam, as the opportunity furnished now may perhaps never present itself again, in the name of what is dearest to you, grant me what I ask."

There was such a tone of respectful prayer in George's voice that Mary turned to the young girl, and, making her a friendly sign with her hand—

"Go, then, darling," said she; "but be easy, you will lose nothing by not hearing. Go."

Mary Seyton withdrew; the queen smilingly looked after her, till the door was shut; then, turning to George—

"Now, sir," said she, "we are alone, speak."

But George, instead of replying, advanced to the queen, and, kneeling on one knee, drew from his breast a paper which he presented to her. Mary took it with amazement, unfolded it, glancing at Douglas, who remained in the same posture, and read as follows:

We, earls, lords, and barons, in consideration that our queen is detained at Lochleven, and that her faithful subjects cannot have access to her person; seeing, on the other hand, that our duty pledges us to provide for her safety, promise and swear to employ all reasonable means which will depend on us to set her at liberty again on conditions compatible with the honour of her Majesty, the welfare of the kingdom, and even with the safety of those who keep her in prison, provided that they consent to give her up; that if they refuse, we declare that we are prepared to make use of ourselves, our children, our friends, our servants, our vassals, our goods, our persons, and our lives, to restore her to liberty, to procure the safety of the prince, and to co-operate in punishing the late king's murderers. If we are assailed for this intent, whether as a body or in private, we promise to defend ourselves, and to aid one another, under pain of infamy and perjury. So may God help us.

"Given with our own hands at Dumbarton,

"St. Andrews, Argyll, Huntly, Arbroath, Galloway, Ross, Fleming, Herries, Stirling, Kilwinning, Hamilton, and Saint-Clair, Knight."

"And Seyton!" cried Mary, "among all these signatures, I do not see that of my faithful Seyton."

Douglas, still kneeling, drew from his breast a second paper, and presented it to the queen with the same marks of respect. It contained only these few words:

"Trust George Douglas; for your Majesty has no more devoted friend in the entire kingdom. "SEYTON."

Mary lowered her eyes to Douglas with an expression which was hers only; then, giving him her hand to raise him—

"Ah!" said she, with a sigh more of joy than of sadness, "now I see that God, in spite of my faults, has not yet abandoned me. But how is it, in this castle, that you, a Douglas.... oh! it is incredible!"

"Madam," replied George, "seven years have passed since I saw you in France for the first time, and for seven years I have loved you". Mary moved; but Douglas put forth his hand and shook his head with an air of such profound sadness, that she understood that she might hear what the young man had to say. He continued: "Reassure yourself, madam; I should never have made this confession if, while explaining my conduct to you, this confession would not have given you greater confidence in me. Yes, for seven years I have loved you, but as one loves a star that one can never reach, a madonna to whom one can only pray; for seven years I have followed you everywhere without you ever having paid attention to me, without my saying a word or making a gesture to attract your notice. I was on the knight of Mevillon's galley when you crossed to Scotland; I was among the regent's soldiers when you beat Huntly; I was in the escort which accompanied you when you went to see the sick king at Glasgow; I reached Edinburgh an hour after you had left it for Lochleven; and then it seemed to me that my mission was revealed to me for the first time, and that this love for which till then, I had reproached myself as a crime, was on the contrary a favour from God. I learned that the lords were assembled at Dumbarton: I flew thither. I pledged my name, I pledged my honour, I pledged my life; and I obtained from them, thanks to the facility I had for coming into this fortress, the happiness of bringing you the paper they have just signed.

Now, madam, forget all I have told you, except the assurance of my devotion and respect: forget that I am near you; I am used to not being seen: only, if you have need of my life, make a sign; for seven years my life has been yours."

"Alas!" replied Mary, "I was complaining this morning of no longer being loved, and I ought to complain, on the contrary, that I am still loved; for the love that I inspire is fatal and mortal. Look back, Douglas, and count the tombs that, young as I am, I have already left on my path—Francis II, Chatelard, Rizzio, Darnley.... Oh to attach one's self to my fortunes more than love is needed now heroism and devotion are requisite so much the more that, as you have said, Douglas, it is love without any possible reward. Do you understand?"

"Oh, madam, madam," answered Douglas, "is it not reward beyond my deserts to see you daily, to cherish the hope that liberty will be restored to you through me, and to have at least, if I do not give it you, the certainty of dying in your sight?"

"Poor young man!" murmured Mary, her eyes raised to heaven, as if she were reading there beforehand the fate awaiting her new defender.

"Happy Douglas, on the contrary," cried George, seizing the queen's hand and kissing it with perhaps still more respect than love, "happy Douglas! for in obtaining a sigh from your Majesty he has already obtained more than he hoped."

"And upon what have you decided with my friends?" said the queen, raising Douglas, who till then had remained on his knees before her.

"Nothing yet," George replied; "for we scarcely had time to see one another. Your escape, impossible without me, is difficult even with me; and your Majesty has seen that I was obliged publicly to fail in respect, to obtain from my mother the confidence which gives me the good fortune of seeing you to-day: if this confidence on my mother's or my brother's part ever extends to giving up to me the castle keys, then you are saved! Let your Majesty not be surprised at anything, then: in the presence of others, I shall ever be always a Douglas, that is an enemy; and except your life be in danger, madam, I shall not utter a word, I shall not make a gesture which might betray the faith that I have sworn you; but, on your side, let your grace know well, that present or absent, whether I am silent or speak, whether I act or remain inert, all will be in appearance only, save my devotion. Only," continued Douglas, approaching the window and showing to the queen a little house on Kinross hill,—"only, look every evening in that direction, madam, and so long as you see a light shine there, your friends will be keeping watch for you, and you need not lose hope."

"Thanks, Douglas, thanks," said the queen; "it does one good to meet with a heart like yours from time to time—oh! thanks."

"And now, madam," replied the young man, "I must leave your Majesty; to remain longer with you would be to raise suspicions, and a single doubt of me, think of it well, madam, and that light which is your sole beacon is extinguished, and all returns into night."

With these words, Douglas bowed more respectfully than he had yet done, and withdrew, leaving Mary full of hope, and still more full of pride; for this time the homage that she had just received was certainly for the woman and not for the queen.

As the queen had told him, Mary Seyton was informed of everything, even the love of Douglas, and, the two women impatiently awaited the evening to see if the promised star would shine on the horizon. Their hope was not in vain: at the appointed time the beacon was lit. The queen trembled with joy, for it was the confirmation of her hopes, and her companion could not tear her from the window, where she remained with her gaze fastened on the little house in Kinross. At last she yielded to Mary Seyton's prayers, and consented to go to bed; but twice in the night she rose noiselessly to go to the window: the light was always shining, and was not extinguished till dawn, with its sisters the stars.

Next day, at breakfast, George announced to the queen the return of his brother, William Douglas: he arrived the same evening; as to himself, George, he had to leave Lochleven next morning, to confer with the nobles who had signed the declaration, and who had immediately separated to raise troops in their several counties. The queen could not attempt to good purpose any escape but at a time when she would be sure of gathering round her an army strong enough to hold the country; as to him, Douglas, one was so used to his silent disappearances and to his unexpected returns, that there was no reason to fear that his departure would inspire any suspicion.

All passed as George had said: in the evening the sound of a bugle announced the arrival of William Douglas; he had with him Lord Ruthven, the son of him who had assassinated Rizzio, and who, exiled with Morton after the murder, died in England of the sickness with which he was already attacked the day of the terrible catastrophe in which we have seen him take such a large share. He preceded by one day Lord Lindsay of Byres and Sir Robert Melville, brother of Mary's former ambassador to Elizabeth: all three were charged with a mission from the regent to the queen.

On the following day everything fell back into the usual routine, and William Douglas reassumed his duties as carver. Breakfast passed without Mary's having learned anything of George's departure or Ruthven's arrival. On rising from the table she went to her window: scarcely was she there than she heard the sound of a horn echoing on the shores of the lake, and saw a little troop of horsemen halt, while waiting for the boat to came and take those who were going to the castle.

The distance was too great for Mary to recognise any of the visitors; but it was clear, from the signs of intelligence exchanged between the little troop and the inhabitants of the fortress, that the newcomers were her enemies. This was a reason why the queen, in her uneasiness, should not lose sight for a moment of the boat which was going to fetch them. She saw only two men get into it; and immediately it put off again for the castle.

As the boat drew nearer, Mary's presentiments changed to real fears, for in one of the men coming towards her she thought she made out Lord Lindsay of Byres, the same who, a week before, had brought her to her prison. It was indeed he himself, as usual in a steel helmet without a visor, which allowed one to see his coarse face designed to express strong passions, and his long black beard with grey hairs here and there, which covered his chest: his person was protected, as if it were in time of war, with his faithful suit of armour, formerly polished and well gilded, but which, exposed without ceasing to rain and mist, was now eaten up with rust; he had slung on his back, much as one slings a quiver, a broadsword, so heavy that it took two hands to manage it, and so long that while the hilt reached the left shoulder the point reached the right spur: in a word, he was still the same soldier, brave to rashness but brutal to insolence, recognising nothing but right and force, and always ready to use force when he believed himself in the right.

The queen was so much taken up with the sight of Lord Lindsay of Byres, that it was only just as the boat reached the shore that she glanced at his companion and recognised Robert Melville: this was some consolation, for, whatever might happen, she knew that she should find in him if not ostensible at least secret sympathy. Besides, his dress, by which one could have judged him equally with Lord Lindsay, was a perfect contrast to his companion's. It consisted of a black velvet doublet, with a cap and a feather of the same hue fastened to it with a gold clasp; his only weapon, offensive or defensive, was a little sword, which he seemed to wear rather as a sign of his rank than for attack or defence. As to his features and his manners, they were in harmony with this peaceful appearance: his pale countenance expressed both acuteness and intelligence; his quick eye was mild, and his voice insinuating; his figure slight and a little bent by habit rather than by years, since he was but forty-five at this time, indicated an easy and conciliatory character.

However, the presence of this man of peace, who seemed entrusted with watching over the demon of war, could not reassure the queen, and as to get to the landing-place, in front of the great door of the castle, the boat had just disappeared behind the corner of a tower, she told Mary Seyton to go down that she might try to learn what cause brought Lord Lindsay to Lochleven, well knowing that with the force of character with which she was endowed, she need know this cause but a few minutes beforehand, whatever it might be, to give her countenance that calm and that majesty which she had always found to influence her enemies.

Left alone, Mary let her glance stray back to the little house in Kinross, her sole hope; but the distance was too great to distinguish anything; besides, its shutters remained closed all day, and seemed to open only in the evening, like the clouds, which, having covered the sky for a whole morning, scatter at last to reveal to the lost sailor a solitary star. She had remained no less motionless, her gaze always fixed on the same object, when she was drawn from this mute contemplation by the step of Mary Seyton.

"Well, darling?" asked the queen, turning round.

"Your Majesty is not mistaken," replied the messenger: "it really was Sir Robert Melville and Lord Lindsay; but there came yesterday with Sir William Douglas a third ambassador, whose name, I am afraid, will be still more odious to your Majesty than either of the two I have just pronounced."

"You deceive yourself, Mary," the queen answered: "neither the name of Melville nor that of Lindsay is odious to me. Melville's, on the contrary, is, in my present circumstances, one of those which I have most pleasure in hearing; as to Lord Lindsay's, it is doubtless not agreeable to me, but it is none the less an honourable name, always borne by men rough and wild, it is true, but incapable of treachery. Tell me, then, what is this name, Mary; for you see I am calm and prepared."

"Alas! madam," returned Mary, "calm and prepared as you may be, collect all your strength, not merely to hear this name uttered, but also to receive in a few minutes the man who bears it; for this name is that of Lord Ruthven."

Mary Seyton had spoken truly, and this name had a terrible influence upon the queen; for scarcely had it escaped the young girl's lips than Mary Stuart uttered a cry, and turning pale, as if she were about to faint, caught hold of the window-ledge.

Mary Seyton, frightened at the effect produced by this fatal name, immediately sprang to support the queen; but she, stretching one hand towards her, while she laid the other on her heart—

"It is nothing," said she; "I shall be better in a moment. Yes, Mary, yes, as you said, it is a fatal name and mingled with one of my most bloody memories. What such men are coming to ask of me must be dreadful indeed. But no matter, I shall soon be ready to receive my brother's ambassadors, for doubtless they are sent in his name. You, darling, prevent their entering, for I must have some minutes to myself: you know me; it will not take me long."

With these words the queen withdrew with a firm step to her bedchamber.

Mary Seyton was left alone, admiring that strength of character which made of Mary Stuart, in all other respects so completely woman-like, a man in the hour of danger. She immediately went to the door to close it with the wooden bar that one passed between two iron rings, but the bar had been taken away, so that there was no means of fastening the door from within. In a moment she heard someone coming up the stairs, and guessing from the heavy, echoing step that this must be Lord Lindsay, she looked round her once again to see if she could find something to replace the bar, and finding nothing within reach, she passed her arm through the rings, resolved to let it be broken rather than allow anyone to approach her mistress before it suited her. Indeed, hardly had those who were coming up reached the landing than someone knocked violently, and a harsh voice cried:

"Come, come, open the door; open directly."

"And by what right," said Mary Seyton, "am I ordered

thus insolently to open the Queen of Scotland's door?"

"By the right of the ambassador of the regent to enter everywhere in his name. I am Lord Lindsay, and I am come to speak to Lady Mary Stuart."

"To be an ambassador," answered Mary Seyton, "is not to be exempted from having oneself announced in visiting a woman, and much more a queen; and if this ambassador is, as he says, Lord Lindsay, he will await his sovereign's leisure, as every Scottish noble would do in his place."

"By St. Andrew!" cried Lord Lindsay, "open, or I will break in the door."

"Do nothing to it, my lord, I entreat you," said another voice, which Mary recognised as Meville's. "Let us rather wait for Lord Ruthven, who is not yet ready."

"Upon my soul," cried Lindsay, shaking the door, "I shall not wait a second". Then, seeing that it resisted, "Why did you tell me, then, you scamp," Lindsay went on, speaking to the steward, "that the bar had been removed?"

"It is true," replied he.

"Then," returned Lindsay, "with what is this silly wench securing the door?"

"With my arm, my lord, which I have passed through the rings, as a Douglas did for King James I, at a time when Douglases had dark hair instead of red, and were faithful instead of being traitors."

"Since you know your history so well," replied Lindsay, in a rage," you should remember that that weak barrier did not hinder Graham, that Catherine Douglas's arm was broken like a willow wand, and that James I was killed like a dog."

"But you, my lord," responded the courageous young girl, "ought also to know the ballad that is still sung in our time—

"'Now, on Robert Gra'am, The king's destroyer, shame! To Robert Graham cling Shame, who destroyed our king.'"

"Mary," cried the queen, who had overheard this altercation from her bedroom,—"Mary, I command you to open the door directly: do you hear?"

Mary obeyed, and Lord Lindsay entered, followed by Melville, who walked behind him, with slow steps and bent head. Arrived in the middle of the second room, Lord Lindsay stopped, and, looking round him—

"Well, where is she, then?" he asked; "and has she not already kept us waiting long enough outside, without making us wait again inside? Or does she imagine that, despite these walls and these bars, she is always queen?"

"Patience, my lord," murmured Sir Robert: "you see that Lord Ruthven has not come yet, and since we can do nothing without him, let us wait."

"Let wait who will," replied Lindsay, inflamed with anger; "but it will not be I, and wherever she may be, I shall go and seek her."

With these words, he made some steps towards Mary Stuart's bedroom; but at the same moment the queen opened the door, without seeming moved either at the visit or at the insolence of the visitors, and so lovely and so full of majesty, that each, even Lindsay himself, was silent at her appearance, and, as if in obedience to a higher power, bowed respectfully before her.

"I fear I have kept you waiting, my lord," said the queen, without replying to the ambassador's salutation otherwise than by a slight inclination of the head; "but a woman does not like to receive even enemies without having spent a few minutes over her toilet. It is true that men are less tenacious of ceremony," added she, throwing a significant glance at Lord Lindsay's rusty armour and soiled and pierced doublet. "Good day, Melville," she continued, without paying attention to some words of excuse stammered by Lindsay; "be welcome in my prison, as you were in my palace; for I believe you as devoted to the one as to the other".

Then, turning to Lindsay, who was looking interrogatively at the door, impatient as he was for Ruthven to come—

"You have there, my lord," said she, pointing to the sword he carried over his shoulder, "a faithful companion, though it is a little heavy: did you expect, in coming here, to find enemies against whom to employ it? In the contrary case, it is a strange ornament for a lady's presence. But no matter, my lord, I, am too much of a Stuart to fear the sight of a sword, even if it were naked, I warn you."

"It is not out of place here, madam," replied Lindsay, bringing it forward and leaning his elbow on its cross hilt, "for it is an old acquaintance of your family."

"Your ancestors, my lord, were brave and loyal enough for me not to refuse to believe what you tell me. Besides, such a good blade must have rendered them good service."

"Yes, madam, yes, surely it has done so, but that kind of

service that kings do not forgive. He for whom it was made was Archibald Bell-the-Cat, and he girded himself with it the day when, to justify his name, he went to seize in the very tent of King James III, your grandfather, his un worthy favourites, Cochran, Hummel, Leonard, and Torpichen, whom he hanged on Louder Bridge with the halters of his soldiers' horses. It was also with this sword that he slew at one blow, in the lists, Spens of Kilspindie, who had insulted him in the presence of King James IV, counting on the protection his master accorded him, and which did not guard him against it any more than his shield, which it split in two. At his master's death, which took place two years after the defeat of Flodden, on whose battlefield he left his two sons and two hundred warriors of the name of Douglas, it passed into the hands of the Earl of Angus, who drew it from the scabbard when he drove the Hamiltons out of Edinburgh, and that so quickly and completely that the affair was called the 'sweeping of the streets.' Finally, your father James V saw it glisten in the fight of the bridge over the Tweed, when Buccleuch, stirred up by him, wanted to snatch him from the guardianship of the Douglases, and when eighty warriors of the name of Scott remained on the battlefield."

"But," said the queen, "how is it that this weapon, after such exploits, has not remained as a trophy in the Douglas family? No doubt the Earl of Angus required a great occasion to decide him to-renounce in your favour this modern Excalibur". [History of Scotland, by Sir Walter Scott.—"The Abbott": historical part.]

"Yes, no doubt, madam, it was upon a great occasion," replied Lindsay, in spite of the imploring signs made by Melville, "and this will have at least the advantage of the others, in being sufficiently recent for you to remember. It was ten days ago, on the battlefield of Carberry Hill, madam, when the infamous Bothwell had the audacity to make a public challenge in which he defied to single combat whomsoever would dare to maintain that he was not innocent of the murder of the king your husband. I made him answer then, I the third, that he was an assassin. And as he refused to fight with the two others under the pretext that they were only barons, I presented myself in my turn, I who am earl and lord. It was on that occasion that the noble Earl of Morton gave me this good sword to fight him to the death. So that, if he had been a little more presumptuous or a little less cowardly, dogs and vultures would be eating at this moment the pieces that, with the help of this good sword, I should have carved for them from that traitor's carcass."

At these words, Mary Seyton and Robert Melville looked at each other in terror, for the events that they recalled were so recent that they were, so to speak, still living in the queen's heart; but the queen, with incredible impassibility and a smile of contempt on her lips—

"It is easy, my lord," said she, "to vanquish an enemy who does not appear in the lists; however, believe me, if Mary had inherited the Stuarts' sword as she has inherited their sceptre, your sword, long as it is, would yet have seemed to you too short. But as you have only to relate to us now, my lord, what you intended doing, and not what you have done, think it fit that I bring you back to something of more reality; for I do not suppose you have given yourself the trouble to come here purely and simply to add a chapter to the little treatise Des Rodomontades Espagnolles by M. de Brantome."

"You are right, madam," replied Lindsay, reddening with anger, "and you would already know the object of our mission if Lord Ruthven did not so ridiculously keep us waiting. But," added he, "have patience; the matter will not be long now, for here he is."

Indeed, at that moment they heard steps mounting the staircase and approaching the room, and at the sound of these steps, the queen, who had borne with such firmness Lindsay's insults, grew so perceptibly paler, that Melville, who did not take his eyes off her,—put out his hand towards the arm-chair as if to push it towards her; but the queen made a sign that she had no need of it, and gazed at the door with apparent calm. Lord Ruthven appeared; it was the first time that she had seen the son since Rizzio had been assassinated by the father.

Lord Ruthven was both a warrior and a statesman, and at this moment his dress savoured of the two professions: it consisted of a close coat of embroidered buff leather, elegant enough to be worn as a court undress, and on which, if need were, one could buckle a cuirass, for battle: like his father, he was pale; like his father, he was to die young, and, even more than his father, his countenance wore that ill-omened melancholy by which fortune-tellers recognise those who are to die a violent death.

Lord Ruthven united in himself the polished dignity of a courtier and the inflexible character of a minister; but quite resolved as he was to obtain from Mary Stuart, even if it were by violence, what he had come to demand in the regent's name, he none the less made her, on entering, a cold but respectful greeting, to which the queen responded with a courtesy; then the steward drew up to the empty arm-chair a heavy table on which had been prepared everything necessary for writing, and at a sign from the two lords he went out, leaving the queen and her companion alone with the three ambassadors. Then the queen, seeing that this table and this arm-chair were put ready for her, sat down; and after a moment, herself breaking this silence more gloomy than any word could have been—

"My lords," said she, "you see that I wait: can it be that this message which you have to communicate to me is so terrible that two soldiers as renowned as Lord Lindsay and Lord Ruthven hesitate at the moment of transmitting it?"

"Madam," answered Ruthven, "I am not of a family, as you know, which ever hesitates to perform a duty, painful as it may be; besides, we hope that your captivity has prepared you to hear what we have to tell you on the part of the Secret Council."

"The Secret Council!" said the queen. "Instituted by me, by what right does it act without me? No matter, I am waiting for this message: I suppose it is a petition to implore my mercy for the men who have dared to reach to a power that I hold only from God."

"Madam," replied Ruthven, who appeared to have undertaken the painful role of spokesman, while Lindsay, mute and impatient, fidgeted with the hilt of his long sword, "it is distressing to me to have to undeceive you on this point: it is not your mercy that I come to ask; it is, on the contrary, the pardon of the Secret Council that I come to offer you."

"To me, my lord, to me!" cried Mary: "subjects offer pardon to their queen! Oh! it is such a new and wonderful thing, that my amazement outweighs my indignation, and that I beg you to continue, instead of stopping you there, as perhaps I ought to do."

"And I obey you so much the more willingly, madam," went on Ruthven imperturbably, "that this pardon is only granted on certain conditions, stated in these documents, destined to re-establish the tranquillity of the State, so cruelly compromised by the errors that they are going to repair."

"And shall I be permitted, my lord, to read these documents, or must I, allured by my confidence in those who present them to me, sign them with my eyes shut?"

"No, madam," Ruthven returned; "the Secret Council desire, on the contrary, that you acquaint yourself with them, for you must sign them freely."

"Read me these documents, my lord; for such a reading is, I think, included in the strange duties you have accepted."

Lord Ruthven took one of the two papers that he had in his hand, and read with the impassiveness of his usual voice the following:

"Summoned from my tenderest youth to the government of the kingdom and to the crown of Scotland, I have carefully attended to the administration; but I have experienced so much fatigue and trouble that I no longer find my mind free enough nor my strength great enough to support the burden of affairs of State: accordingly, and as Divine favour has granted us a son whom we desire to see during our lifetime bear the crown which he has acquired by right of birth, we have resolved to abdicate, and we abdicate in his favour, by these presents, freely and voluntarily, all our rights to the crown and to the government of Scotland, desiring that he may immediately ascend the throne, as if he were called to it by our natural death, and not as the effect of our own will; and that our present abdication may have a more complete and solemn effect, and that no one should put forward the claim of ignorance, we give full powers to our trusty and faithful cousins, the lords Lindsay of Byres and William Ruthven, to appear in our name before the nobility, the clergy, and the burgesses of Scotland, of whom they will convoke an assembly at Stirling, and to there renounce, publicly and solemnly, on our part, all our claims to the crown and to the government of Scotland.

"Signed freely and as the testimony of one of our last royal wishes, in our castle of Lochleven, the ___ June 1567". (The date was left blank.)

There was a moment's silence after this reading, then "Did you hear, madam?" asked Ruthven.

"Yes," replied Mary Stuart,—"yes, I have heard rebellious

words that I have not understood, and I thought that my ears, that one has tried to accustom for some time to a strange language, still deceived me, and that I have thought for your honour, my lord William Ruthven, and my lord Lindsay of Byres."

"Madam," answered Lindsay, out of patience at having kept silence so long, "our honour has nothing to do with the opinion of a woman who has so ill known how to watch over her own."

"My lord!" said Melville, risking a word.

"Let him speak, Robert," returned the queen. "We have in our conscience armour as well tempered as that with which Lord Lindsay is so prudently covered, although, to the shame of justice, we no longer have a sword. Continue, my lord," the queen went on, turning to Lord Ruthven: "is this all that my subjects require of me? A date and a signature? Ah! doubtless it is too little; and this second paper, which you have kept in order to proceed by degrees, probably contains some demand more difficult to grant than that of yielding to a child scarcely a year old a crown which belongs to me by birthright, and to abandon my sceptre to take a distaff."

"This other paper," replied Ruthven, without letting himself be intimidated by the tone of bitter irony adopted by the queen, "is the deed by which your Grace confirms the decision of the Secret Council which has named your beloved brother, the Earl of Murray, regent of the kingdom."

"Indeed!" said Mary. "The Secret Council thinks it needs my confirmation to an act of such slight importance? And my beloved brother, to bear it without remorse, needs that it should be I who add a fresh title to those of Earl of Mar and of Murray that I have already bestowed upon him? But one cannot desire anything more respectful and touching than all this, and I should be very wrong to complain. My lords," continued the queen, rising and changing her tone, "return to those who have sent you, and tell them that to such demands Mary Stuart has no answer to give."

"Take care, madam," responded Ruthven; "for I have told you it is only on these conditions that your pardon can be granted you."

"And if I refuse this generous pardon," asked Mary, "what will happen?"

"I cannot pronounce beforehand, madam; but your Grace has enough knowledge of the laws, and above all of the history of Scotland and England, to know that murder and adultery are crimes for which more than one queen has been punished with death."

"And upon what proofs could such a charge be founded, my lord? Pardon my persistence, which takes up your precious time; but I am sufficiently interested in the matter to be permitted such a question."

"The proof, madam?" returned Ruthven. "There is but one, I know; but that one is unexceptionable: it is the precipitate marriage of the widow of the assassinated with the chief assassin, and the letters which have been handed over to us by James Balfour, which prove that the guilty persons had united their adulterous hearts before it was permitted them to unite their bloody hands."

"My lord," cried the queen, "do you forget a certain repast given in an Edinburgh tavern, by this same Bothwell, to those same noblemen who treat him to-day as an adulterer and a murderer; do you forget that at the end of that meal, and on the same table at which it had been given, a paper was signed to invite that same woman, to whom to-day you make the haste of her new wedding a crime, to leave off a widow's mourning to reassume a marriage robe? for if you have forgotten it, my lords, which would do no more honour to your sobriety than to your memory, I undertake to show it to you, I who have preserved it; and perhaps if we search well we shall find among the signatures the names of Lindsay of Byres and William Ruthven. O noble Lord Herries," cried Mary, "loyal James Melville, you alone were right then, when you threw yourselves at my feet, entreating me not to conclude this marriage, which, I see it clearly to-day, was only a trap set for an ignorant woman by perfidious advisers or disloyal lords."

"Madam," cried Ruthven, in spite of his cold impassivity beginning to lose command of himself, while Lindsay was giving still more noisy and less equivocal signs of impatience, "madam, all these discussions are beside our aim: I beg you to return to it, then, and inform us if, your life and honour guaranteed, you consent to abdicate the crown of Scotland."

"And what safeguard should I have that the promises you here make me will be kept?"

"Our word, madam," proudly replied Ruthven.

"Your word, my lord, is a very feeble pledge to offer, when one so quickly forgets one's signature: have you not some trifle to add to it, to make me a little easier than I should be with it alone?"

"Enough, Ruthven, enough," cried Lindsay. "Do you not see that for an hour this woman answers our proposals only by insults?"

"Yes, let us go," said Ruthven; "and thank yourself only, madam, for the day when the thread breaks which holds the sword suspended over your head."

"My lords," cried Melville, "my lords, in Heaven's name, a little patience, and forgive something to her who, accustomed to command, is today forced to obey."

"Very well," said Lindsay, turning round, "stay with her, then, and try to obtain by your smooth words what is refused to our frank and loyal demand. In a quarter of an hour we shall return: let the answer be ready in a quarter of an hour!"

With these words, the two noblemen went out, leaving Melville with the queen; and one could count their footsteps, from the noise that Lindsay's great sword made, in resounding on each step of the staircase.

Scarcely were they alone than Melville threw himself at the queen's feet.

"Madam," said he, "you remarked just now that Lord Herries and my brother had given your Majesty advice that you repented not having followed; well, madam, reflect on that I in my turn give you; for it is more important than the other, for you will regret with still more bitterness not having listened to it. Ah! you do not know what may happen, you are ignorant of what your brother is capable."

"It seems to me, however," returned the queen, "that he has just instructed me on that head: what more will he do than he has done already? A public trial! Oh! it is all I ask: let me only plead my cause, and we shall see what judges will dare to condemn me."

"But that is what they will take good care not to do, madam; for they would be mad to do it when they keep you here in this isolated castle, in the care of your enemies, having no witness but God, who avenges crime, but who does not prevent it. Recollect, madam, what Machiavelli has said, 'A king's tomb is never far from his prison.' You come of a family in which one dies young, madam, and almost always of a sudden death: two of your ancestors perished by steel, and one by poison."

"Oh, if my death were sudden and easy," cried Mary, "yes, I should accept it as an expiation for my faults; for if I am proud when I compare myself with others, Melville, I am humble when I judge myself. I am unjustly accused of being an accomplice of Darnley's death, but I am justly condemned for having married Bothwell."

"Time presses, madam; time presses," cried Melville, looking at the sand, which, placed on the table, was marking the time. "They are coming back, they will be here in a minute; and this time you must give them an answer. Listen, madam, and at least profit by your situation as much as you can. You are alone here with one woman, without friends, without protection, without power: an abdication signed at such a juncture will never appear to your people to have been freely given, but will always pass as having been torn from you by force; and if need be, madam, if the day comes when such a solemn declaration is worth something, well, then you will have two witnesses of the violence done you: the one will be Mary Seyton, and the other," he added in a low voice and looking uneasily about him,—"the other will be Robert Melville."

Hardly had he finished speaking when the footsteps of the two nobles were again heard on the staircase, returning even before the quarter of an hour had elapsed; a moment afterwards the door opened, and Ruthven appeared, while over his shoulder was seen Lindsay's head.

"Madam," said Ruthven, "we have returned. Has your Grace decided? We come for your answer."

"Yes," said Lindsay, pushing aside Ruthven, who stood in his way, and advancing to the table,—"yes, an answer, clear, precise, positive, and without dissimulation."

"You are exacting, my lord," said the queen: "you would scarcely have the right to expect that from me if I were in full liberty on the other side of the lake and surrounded with a faithful escort; but between these walls, behind these bars, in the depths of this fortress, I shall not tell you that I sign voluntarily, lest you should not believe it. But no matter, you want my signature; well, I am going to give it to you. Melville, pass me the pen."

"But I hope," said Lord Ruthven, "that your Grace is not

counting on using your present position one day in argument to protest against what you are going to do?"

The queen had already stooped to write, she had already set her hand to the paper, when Ruthven spoke to her. But scarcely had he done so, than she rose up proudly, and letting fall the pen, "My lord," said she, "what you asked of me just now was but an abdication pure and simple, and I was going to sign it. But if to this abdication is joined this marginal note, then I renounce of my own accord, and as judging myself unworthy, the throne of Scotland. I would not do it for the three united crowns that I have been robbed of in turn."

"Take care, madam," cried Lord Lindsay, seizing the queen's wrist with his steel gauntlet and squeezing it with all his angry strength—"take care, for our patience is at an end, and we could easily end by breaking what would not bend."

The queen remained standing, and although a violent flush had passed like a flame over her countenance, she did not utter a word, and did not move: her eyes only were fixed with such a great expression of contempt on those of the rough baron, that he, ashamed of the passion that had carried him away, let go the hand he had seized and took a step back. Then raising her sleeve and showing the violet marks made on her arm by Lord Lindsay's steel gauntlet.

"This is what I expected, my lords," said she, "and nothing prevents me any longer from signing; yes, I freely abdicate the throne and crown of Scotland, and there is the proof that my will has not been forced."

With these words, she took the pen and rapidly signed the two documents, held them out to Lord Ruthven, and bowing with great dignity, withdrew slowly into her room, accompanied by Mary Seyton. Ruthven looked after her, and when she had disappeared, "It doesn't matter," he said; "she has signed, and although the means you employed, Lindsay, may be obsolete enough in diplomacy, it is not the less efficacious, it seems."

"No joking, Ruthven," said Lindsay; "for she is a noble creature, and if I had dared, I should have thrown myself at her feet to ask her forgiveness."

"There is still time," replied Ruthven, "and Mary, in her present situation, will not be severe upon you: perhaps she has resolved to appeal to the judgment of God to prove her innocence, and in that case a champion such as you might well change the face of things."

"Do not joke, Ruthven," Lindsay answered a second time, with more violence than the first; "for if I were as well convinced of her innocence as I am of her crime, I tell you that no one should touch a hair of her head, not even the regent."

"The devil! my lord," said Ruthven. "I did not know you were so sensitive to a gentle voice and a tearful eye; you know the story of Achilles' lance, which healed with its rust the wounds it made with its edge: do likewise my lord, do likewise."

"Enough, Ruthven, enough," replied Lindsay; "you are like a corselet of Milan steel, which is three times as bright as the steel armour of Glasgow, but which is at the same time thrice as hard: we know one another, Ruthven, so an end to railleries or threats; enough, believe me, enough."

And after these words, Lord Lindsay went out first, followed by Ruthven and Melville, the first with his head high and affecting an air of insolent indifference, and the second, sad, his brow bent, and not even trying to disguise the painful impression which this scene had made on him.' ["History of Scotland, by Sir Walter Scott.—'The Abbott": historical part.]

CHAPTER VI

The queen came out of her room only in the evening, to take her place at the window which looked over the lake: at the usual time she saw the light which was henceforth her sole hope shine in the little house in Kinross; for a whole long month she had no other consolation than seeing it, every night, fixed and faithful.

At last, at the end of this time, and as she was beginning to despair of seeing George Douglas again, one morning, on opening the window, she uttered a cry. Mary Seyton ran to her, and the queen, without having strength to speak, showed her in the middle of the lake the tiny boat at anchor, and in the boat Little Douglas and George, who were absorbed in fishing, their favourite amusement. The young man had arrived the day before, and as everyone was accustomed to his unexpected returns, the sentinel had not even blown the horn, and the queen had not known that at last a friend had come.

However, she was three days yet without seeing this friend otherwise than she had just done-that is, on the lake. It is true that from morning till evening he did not leave that spot, from which he could view the queen's windows and the queen herself, when, to gaze at a wider horizon, she leaned her face against the bars. At last, on the morning of the fourth day, the queen was awakened by a great noise of dogs and horns: she immediately ran to the window, for to a prisoner everything is an event, and she saw William Douglas, who was embarking with a pack of hounds and some huntsmen. In fact, making a truce, for a day, with his gaoler's duties, to enjoy a pleasure more in harmony with his rank and birth, he was going to hunt in the woods which cover the last ridge of Ben Lomond, and which, ever sinking, die down on the banks of the lake.

The queen trembled with delight, for she hoped that Lady Lochleven would maintain her ill-will, and that then George would replace his brother: this hope was not disappointed. At the usual time the queen heard the footsteps of those who were bringing her her breakfast; the door opened, and she saw George Douglas enter, preceded by the servants who were carrying the dishes. George barely bowed; but the queen, warned by him not to be surprised at anything, returned him his greeting with a disdainful air; then the servants performed their task and went out, as they were accustomed.

"At last," said the queen, "you are back again, then."

George motioned with his finger, went to the door to listen if all the servants had really gone away, and if no one had remained to spy. Then, returning more at ease, and bowing respectfully—

"Yes, madam," returned he; "and, Heaven be thanked, I bring good news."

"Oh, tell me quickly!" cried the queen; "for staying in this castle is hell. You knew that they came, did you not, and that they made me sign an abdication?"

"Yes, madam," replied Douglas; "but we also knew that

your signature had been obtained from you by violence alone, and our devotion to your Majesty is increased thereby, if possible."

"But, after all, what have you done?"

"The Seytons and the Hamiltons, who are, as your Majesty knows, your most faithful servants,"—Mary turned round, smiling, and put out her hand to Mary Seyton,— "have already," continued George, "assembled their troops, who keep themselves in readiness for the first signal; but as they alone would not be sufficiently numerous to hold the country, we shall make our way directly to Dumbarton, whose governor is ours, and which by its position and its strength can hold out long enough against all the regent's troops to give to the faithful hearts remaining to you time to come and join us."

"Yes, yes," said the queen; "I see clearly what we shall do once we get out of this; but how are we to get out?"

"That is the occasion, madam," replied Douglas, "for which your Majesty must call to your aid that courage of which you have given such great proofs."

"If I have need only of courage and coolness," replied the queen, "be easy; neither the one nor the other will fail me."

"Here is a file," said George, giving Mary Seyton that instrument which he judged unworthy to touch the queen's hands, "and this evening I shall bring your Majesty cords to construct a ladder. You will cut through one of the bars of this window, it is only at a height of twenty feet; I shall come up to you, as much to try it as to support you; one of the garrison is in my pay, he will give us passage by the door it is his duty to guard, and you will be free."

"And when will that be?" cried the queen.

"We must wait for two things, madam," replied Douglas: "the first, to collect at Kinross an escort sufficient for your Majesty's safety; the second, that the turn for night watch of Thomas Warden should happen to be at an isolated door that we can reach without being seen."

"And how will you know that? Do you stay at the castle, then?"

"Alas! no, madam," replied George; "at the castle I am a useless and even a dangerous fried for you, while once beyond the lake I can serve you in an effectual manner."

"And how will you know when Warden's turn to mount guard has come?"

"The weathercock in the north tower, instead of turning in the wind with the others, will remain fixed against it."

"But I, how shall I be warned?"

"Everything is already provided for on that side: the light which shines each night in the little house in Kinross incessantly tells you that your friends keep watch for you; but when you would like to know if the hour of your deliverance approaches or recedes, in your turn place a light in this window. The other will immediately disappear; then, placing your hand on your breast, count your heartbeats: if you reach the number twenty without the light reappearing, nothing is yet settled; if you only reach ten, the moment approaches; if the light does not leave you time to count beyond five, your escape is fixed for the following night; if it reappears no more, it is fixed for the same evening; then the owl's cry, repeated thrice in the courtyard, will be the signal; let down the ladder when you hear it".

"Oh, Douglas," cried the queen, "you alone could foresee and calculate everything thus. Thank you, thank you a hundred times!" And she gave him her hand to kiss.

A vivid red flushed the young man's cheeks; but almost directly mastering his emotion, he kneeled down, and, restraining the expression of that love of which he had once spoken to the queen, while promising her never more to speak of it, he took the hand that Mary extended, and kissed it with such respect that no one could have seen in this action anything but the homage of devotion and fidelity.

Then, having bowed to the queen, he went out, that a longer stay with her should not give rise to any suspicions.

At the dinner-hour Douglas brought, as he had said, a parcel of cord. It was not enough, but when evening came Mary Seyton was to unroll it and let fall the end from the window, and George would fasten the remainder to it: the thing was done as arranged, and without any mishap, an hour after the hunters had returned.

The following day George left the castle.

The queen and Mary Seyton lost no time in setting about the rope ladder, and it was finished on the third day. The same evening, the queen in her impatience, and rather to assure herself of her partisans' vigilance than in the hope that the time of her deliverance was so near, brought her lamp to the window: immediately, and as George Douglas had told her, the light in the little house at Kinross disappeared: the queen then laid her hand on her heart and counted up to twenty-two; then the light reappeared; they were ready for everything, but nothing was yet settled. For a week the queen thus questioned the light and her heart-beats without their number changing; at last, on the eighth day, she counted only as far as ten; at the eleventh the light reappeared.

The queen believed herself mistaken: she did not dare to hope what this announced. She withdrew the lamp; then, at the end of a quarter of an hour, showed it again: her unknown correspondent understood with his usual intelligence that a fresh trial was required of him, and the light in the little house disappeared in its turn. Mary again questioned the pulsations of her heart, and, fast as it leaped, before the twelfth beat the propitious star was shining on the horizon: there was no longer any doubt; everything was settled.

Mary could not sleep all night: this persistency of her partisans inspired her with gratitude to the point of tears. The day came, and the queen several times questioned her companion to assure herself that it was not all a dream; at every sound it seemed to her that the scheme on which her liberty hung was discovered, and when, at breakfast and at dinner time, William Douglas entered as usual, she hardly dared look at him, for fear of reading on his face the announcement that all was lost.

In the evening the queen again questioned the light: it made the same answer; nothing had altered; the beacon was always one of hope.

For four days it thus continued to indicate that the moment of escape was at hand; on the evening of the fifth, before the queen had counted five beats, the light reappeared: the queen leaned upon Mary Seyton; she was nearly fainting, between dread and 'delight. Her escape was fixed for the next evening.

The queen tried once more, and obtained the same reply: there was no longer a doubt; everything was ready except the prisoner's courage, for it failed her for a moment, and if Mary Seyton had not drawn up a seat in time, she would have fallen prone; but, the first moment over, she collected herself as usual, and was stronger and more resolute than ever.

Till midnight the queen remained at the window, her eyes fixed on that star of good omen: at last Mary Seyton persuaded her to go to bed, offering, if she had no wish to sleep, to read her some verses by M. Ronsard, or some chapters from the Mer des Histoires; but Mary had no desire now for any profane reading, and had her Hours read, making the responses as she would have done if she had been present at a mass said by a Catholic priest: towards dawn, however, she grew drowsy, and as Mary Seyton, for her part, was dropping with fatigue, she fell asleep directly in the arm-chair at the head of the queen's bed.

Next day she awoke, feeling that someone was tapping her on the shoulder: it was the queen, who had already arisen.

"Come and see, darling," said she,—"come and see the

fine day that God is giving us. Oh! how alive is Nature! How happy I shall be to be once more free among those plains and mountains! Decidedly, Heaven is on our side."

"Madam," replied Mary, "I would rather see the weather less fine: it would promise us a darker night; and consider, what we need is darkness, not light."

"Listen," said the queen; "it is by this we are going to see if God is indeed for us; if the weather remains as it is, yes, you are right, He abandons us; but if it clouds over, oh! then, darling, this will be a certain proof of His protection, will it not?"

Mary Seyton smiled, nodding that she adopted her mistress's superstition; then the queen, incapable of remaining idle in her great preoccupation of mind, collected the few jewels that she had preserved, enclosed them in a casket, got ready for the evening a black dress, in order to be still better hidden in the darkness: and, these preparations made, she sat down again at the window, ceaselessly carrying her eyes from the lake to the little house in Kinross, shut up and dumb as usual.

The dinner-hour arrived: the queen was so happy that she received William Douglas with more goodwill than was her wont, and it was with difficulty she remained seated during the time the meal lasted; but she restrained herself, and William Douglas withdrew, without seeming to have noticed her agitation.

Scarcely had he gone than Mary ran to the window; she had need of air, and her gaze devoured in advance those wide horizons which she was about to cross anew; it seemed to her that once at liberty she would never shut herself up in a palace again, but would wander about the countryside continually: then, amid all these tremors of delight, from time to time she felt unexpectedly heavy at heart. She then turned round to Mary Seyton, trying to fortify her strength with hers, and the young girl kept up her hopes, but rather from duty than from conviction.

But slow as they seemed to the queen, the hours yet passed: towards the afternoon some clouds floated across the blue sky; the queen remarked upon them joyfully to her companion; Mary Seyton congratulated her upon them, not on account of the imaginary omen that the queen sought in them, but because of the real importance that the weather should be cloudy, that darkness might aid them in their flight. While the two prisoners were watching the billowy, moving vapours, the hour of dinner arrived; but it was half an hour of constraint and dissimulation, the more painful that, no doubt in return for the sort of goodwill shown him by the queen in the morning, William Douglas thought himself obliged, in his turn, to accompany his duties with fitting compliments, which compelled the queen to take a more active part in the conversation than her preoccupation allowed her; but William Douglas did not seem in any way to observe this absence of mind, and all passed as at breakfast.

Directly he had gone the queen ran to the window: the few clouds which were chasing one another in the sky an hour before had thickened and spread, and—all the blue was blotted out, to give place to a hue dull and leaden as pewter. Mary Stuart's presentiments were thus realised: as to the little house in Kinross, which one could still make out in the dusk, it remained shut up, and seemed deserted.

Night fell: the light shone as usual; the queen signalled, it disappeared. Mary Stuart waited in vain; everything remained in darkness: the escape was for the same evening. The queen heard eight o'clock, nine o'clock, and ten o'clock strike successively. At ten o'clock the sentinels were relieved; Mary Stuart heard the patrols pass beneath her windows, the steps of the watch recede: then all returned to silence. Half an hour passed away thus; suddenly the owl's cry resounded thrice, the queen recognised George Douglas's signal: the supreme moment had come.

In these circumstances the queen found all her strength revive: she signed to Mary Seyton to take away the bar and to fix the rope ladder, while, putting out the lamp, she felt her way into the bedroom to seek the casket which contained her few remaining jewels. When she came back, George Douglas was already in the room.

"All goes well, madam," said he. "Your friends await you on the other side of the lake, Thomas Warden watches at the postern, and God has sent us a dark night."

The queen, without replying, gave him her hand. George bent his knee and carried this hand to his lips; but on touching it, he felt it cold and trembling.

"Madam," said he, "in Heaven's name summon all your courage, and do not let yourself be downcast at such a moment."

"Our Lady-of-Good-Help," murmured Seyton, "come to our aid!"

"Summon to you the spirit of the kings your ancestors," responded George, "for at this moment it is not the resignation of a Christian that you require, but the strength and resolution of a queen"

"Oh, Douglas! Douglas," cried Mary mournfully, "a fortune-teller predicted to me that I should die in prison and by a violent death: has not the hour of the prediction arrived?"

"Perhaps," George said, "but it is better to die as a queen than to live in this ancient castle calumniated and a prisoner."

"You are right, George," the queen answered; "but for a woman the first step is everything: forgive me". Then, after a moment's pause, "Come," said she; "I am ready."

George immediately went to the window, secured the ladder again and more firmly, then getting up on to the sill and holding to the bars with one hand, he stretched out the other to the queen, who, as resolute as she had been timid a moment before, mounted on a stool, and had already set one foot on the window-ledge, when suddenly the cry, "Who goes there?" rang out at the foot of the tower. The queen sprang quickly back, partly instinctively and partly pushed by George, who, on the contrary, leaned out of the window to see whence came this cry, which, twice again renewed, remained twice unanswered, and was immediately followed by a report and the flash of a firearm: at the same moment the sentinel on duty on the tower blew his bugle, another set going the alarm bell, and the cries, "To arms, to arms!" and "Treason, treason!" resounded throughout the castle.

"Yes, yes, treason, treason!" cried George Douglas, leaping down into the room. "Yes, the infamous Warden has betrayed us!" Then, advancing to Mary, cold and motionless as a statue, "Courage, madam," said he, "courage! Whatever happens, a friend yet remains for you in the castle; it is Little Douglas."

Scarcely had he finished speaking when the door of the queen's apartment opened, and William Douglas and Lady Lochleven, preceded by servants carrying torches and armed soldiers, appeared on the threshold: the room was immediately filled with people and light.

"Mother," said William Douglas, pointing to his brother standing before Mary Stuart and protecting her with his body, "do you believe me now? Look!"

The old lady was for a moment speechless; then finding a word at last, and taking a step forward—

"Speak, George Douglas," cried she, "speak, and clear yourself at once of the charge which weighs on your honour; say but these words, 'A Douglas was never faithless to his trust,' and I believe you".

"Yes, mother," answered William, "a Douglas!... but he— he is not a Douglas."

"May God grant my old age the strength needed to bear on the part of one of my sons such a misfortune, and on the part of the other such an injury!" exclaimed Lady Lochleven. "O woman born under a fatal star," she went on, addressing the queen, "when will you cease to be, in the Devil's hands, an instrument of perdition and death to all who approach you? O ancient house of Lochleven, cursed be the hour when this enchantress crossed thy threshold!"

"Do not say that, mother, do not say that," cried George; "blessed be, on the contrary, the moment which proves that, if there are Douglases who no longer remember what they owe to their sovereigns, there are others who have never forgotten it."

"Douglas! Douglas!" murmured Mary Stuart, "did I not tell you?"

"And I, madam," said George, "what did I reply then? That it was an honour and a duty to every faithful subject of your Majesty to die for you."

"Well, die, then!" cried William Douglas, springing on his brother with raised sword, while he, leaping back, drew his, and with a movement quick as thought and eager as hatred defended himself. But at the same moment Mary Stuart darted between the two young people.

"Not another step, Lord Douglas," said she. "Sheathe your sword, George, or if you use it, let be to go hence, and against everyone but your b other. I still have need of your life; take care of it."

"My life, like my arm and my honour, is at your service, madam, and from the moment you command it I shall preserve it for you."

With these words, rushing to the door with a violence and resolve which prevented anyone's stopping him—

"Back!" cried he to the domestics who were barring the passage; "make way for the young master of Douglas, or woe to you!".

"Stop him!" cried William. "Seize him, dead or alive! Fire upon him! Kill him like a dog!"

Two or three soldiers, not daring to disobey William, pretended to pursue his brother. Then some gunshots were heard, and a voice crying that George Douglas had just thrown himself into the lake.

"And has he then escaped?" cried William.

Mary Stuart breathed again; the old lady raised her hands to Heaven.

"Yes, yes," murmured William,—"yes, thank Heaven for your son's flight; for his flight covers our entire house with shame; counting from this hour, we shall be looked upon as the accomplices of his treason."

"Have pity on me, William!" cried Lady Lochleven, wringing her hands. "Have compassion o your old mother! See you not that I am dying?"

With these words, she fell backwards, pale and tottering; the steward and a servant supported er in their arms.

"I believe, my lord," said Mary Seyton, coming forward, "that your mother has as much need of attention just now as the queen has need of repose: do you not consider it is time for you to withdraw?"

"Yes, yes," said William, "to give you time to spin fresh webs, I suppose, and to seek what fresh flies you can take in them? It is well, go on with your work; but you have just seen that it is not easy to deceive William Douglas. Play your game, I shall play mine". Then turning to the servants, "Go out, all of you," said he; "and you, mother, come."

The servants and the soldiers obeyed; then William Douglas went out last, supporting Lady Lochleven, and the queen heard him shut behind him and double-lock the two doors of her prison.

Scarcely was Mary alone, and certain that she was no longer seen or heard, than all her strength deserted her, and, sinking into an arm-chair, she burst out sobbing.

Indeed, all her courage had been needed to sustain her so far, and the sight of her enemies alone had given her this courage; but hardly had they gone than her situation appeared before her in all its fatal hardship. Dethroned, a prisoner, without another fiend in this impregnable castle than a child to whom she had scarce given attention, and who was the sole and last thread attaching her past hopes to her hopes for the future, what remained to Mary Stuart of her two thrones and her double power? Her name, that was all; her, name with which, free, she had doubtless stirred Scotland, but which little by little was about to be effaced in the hearts of her adherents, and which during her lifetime oblivion was to cover perhaps as with a shroud. Such an idea was insupportable to a soul as lofty as Mary Stuart's, and to an organisation which, like that of the flowers, has need, before everything, of air, light, and sun.

Fortunately there remained to her the best beloved of her four Marys, who, always devoted and consoling, hastened to succour and comfort her; but this time it was no easy matter, and the queen let her act and speak without answering her otherwise than with sobs and tears; when suddenly, looking through the window to which she had drawn up her mistress's armchair—

"The light!" cried she, "madam, the light!"

At the same time she raised the queen, and with arm outstretched from the window, she showed her the beacon, the eternal symbol of hope, relighted in the midst of this dark night on Kinross hill: there was no mistake possible, not a star was shining in the sky.

"Lord God, I give Thee thanks," said the queen, falling on her knees and raising her arms to heaven with a gesture of gratitude: "Douglas has escaped, and my friends still keep watch."

Then, after a fervent prayer, which restored to her a little strength, the queen re-entered her room, and, tired out by her varied successive emotions, she slept an uneasy, agitated sleep, over which the indefatigable Mary Seyton kept watch till daybreak.

As William Douglas had said, from this time forward the queen was a prisoner indeed, and permission to go down into the garden was no longer granted but under the surveillance of two soldiers; but this annoyance seemed to her so unbearable that she preferred to give up the recreation, which, surrounded with such conditions, became a torture. So she shut herself up in her apartments, finding a certain bitter and haughty pleasure in the very excess of her misfortune.

CHAPTER VII

A week after the events we have related, as nine o'clock in the evening had just sounded from the castle bell, and the queen and Mary Seyton were sitting at a table where they were working at their tapestry, a stone thrown from the courtyard passed through the window bars, broke a pane of glass, and fell into the room. The queen's first idea was to believe it accidental or an insult; but Mary Seyton, turning round, noticed that the stone was wrapped up in a paper: she immediately picked it up. The paper was a letter from George Douglas, conceived in these terms:

"You have commanded me to live, madam: I have obeyed, and your Majesty has been able to tell, from the Kinross light, that your servants continue to watch over you. However, not to raise suspicion, the soldiers collected for that fatal night dispersed at dawn, and will not gather again till a fresh attempt makes their presence necessary. But, alas! to renew this attempt now, when your Majesty's gaolers are on their guard, would be your ruin. Let them take every precaution, then, madam; let them sleep in security, while we, we, in our devotion, shall go on watching.

"Patience and courage!"

"Brave and loyal heart!" cried Mary, "more constantly devoted to misfortune than others are to prosperity! Yes, I shall have patience and courage, and so long as that light shines I shall still believe in liberty."

This letter restored to the queen all her former courage:

she had means of communication with George through Little Douglas; for no doubt it was he who had thrown that stone. She hastened, in her turn, to write a letter to George, in which she both charged him to express her gratitude to all the lords who had signed the protestation; and begged them, in the name of the fidelity they had sworn to her, not to cool in their devotion, promising them, for her part, to await the result with that patience and courage they asked of her.

The queen was not mistaken: next day, as she was at her window, Little Douglas came to play at the foot of the tower, and, without raising his head, stopped just beneath her to dig a trap to catch birds. The queen looked to see if she were observed, and assured that that part of the courtyard was deserted, she let fall the stone wrapped in her letter: at first she feared to have made a serious error; for Little Douglas did not even turn at the noise, and it was only after a moment, during which the prisoner's heart was torn with frightful anxiety, that indifferently, and as if he were looking for something else, the child laid his hand on the stone, and without hurrying, without raising his head, without indeed giving any sign of intelligence to her who had thrown it, he put the letter in his pocket, finishing the work he had begun with the greatest calm, and showing the queen, by this coolness beyond his years, what reliance she could place in him.

From that moment the queen regained fresh hope; but days, weeks, months passed without bringing any change in her situation: winter came; the prisoner saw snow spread over the plains and mountains, and the lake afforded her, if she had only been able to pass the door, a firm road to gain the other bank; but no letter came during all this time to bring her the consoling news that they were busy about her deliverance; the faithful light alone announced to her every evening that a friend was keeping watch.

Soon nature awoke from her death-sleep: some forward sun-rays broke through the clouds of this sombre sky of Scotland; the snow melted, the lake broke its ice-crust, the first buds opened, the green turf reappeared; everything came out of its prison at the joyous approach of spring, and it was a great grief to Mary to see that she alone was condemned to an eternal winter.

At last; one evening, she thought she observed in the motions of the light that something fresh was happening: she had so often questioned this poor flickering star, and she had so often let it count her heart-beats more than twenty times, that to spare herself the pain of disappointment, for a long time she had no longer interrogated it; however, she resolved to make one last attempt, and, almost hopeless, she put her light near the window, and immediately took it away; still, faithful to the signal, the other disappeared at the same moment, and reappeared at the eleventh heart-beat of the queen. At the same time, by a strange coincidence, a stone passing through the window fell at Mary Seyton's feet. It was, like the first, wrapped in a letter from George: the queen took it from her companion's hands, opened it, and read:

"The moment draws near; your adherents are assembled;

summon all your courage."

"To-morrow, at eleven o'clock in the evening, drop a cord from your window, and draw up the packet that will be fastened to it."

There remained in the queen's apartments the rope over and above what had served for the ladder taken away by the guards the evening of the frustrated escape: next day, at the appointed hour, the two prisoners shut up the lamp in the bedroom, so that no light should betray them, and Mary Seyton, approaching the window, let down the cord. After a minute, she felt from its movements that something was being attached to it. Mary Seyton pulled, and a rather bulky parcel appeared at the bars, which it could not pass on account of its size. Then the queen came to her companion's aid. The parcel was untied, and its contents, separately, got through easily. The two prisoners carried them into the bedroom, and, barricaded within, commenced an inventory. There were two complete suits of men's clothes in the Douglas livery. The queen was at a loss, when she saw a letter fastened to the collar of one of the two coats. Eager to know the meaning of this enigma, she immediately opened it, and read as follows:

"It is only by dint of audacity that her Majesty can recover her liberty: let her Majesty read this letter, then, and punctually follow, if she deign to adopt them, the instructions she will find therein.

"In the daytime the keys of the castle do not leave the belt of the old steward; when curfew is rung and he has made his rounds to make sure that all the doors are fast shut, he gives them up to William Douglas, who, if he stays up, fastens them to his sword-belt, or, if he sleeps, puts them under his pillow. For five months, Little Douglas, whom everyone is accustomed to see working at the armourer's forge of the castle, has been employed in making some keys like enough to the others, once they are substituted for them, for William to be deceived. Yesterday Little Douglas finished the last.

"On the first favourable opportunity that her Majesty will know to be about to present itself, by carefully questioning the light each day, Little Douglas will exchange the false keys for the true, will enter the queen's room, and will find her dressed, as well as Miss Mary Seyton, in their men's clothing, and he will go before them to lead them, by the way which offers the best chances for their escape; a boat will be prepared and will await them.

"Till then, every evening, as much to accustom themselves to these new costumes as to give them an appearance of having been worn, her Majesty and Miss Mary Seyton will dress themselves in the suits, which they must keep on from nine o'clock till midnight. Besides, it is possible that, without having had time to warn them, their young guide may suddenly come to seek them: it is urgent, then, that he find them ready.

"The garments ought to fit perfectly her Majesty and her companion, the measure having been taken on Miss Mary Fleming and Miss Mary Livingston, who are exactly their size.

"One cannot too strongly recommend her Majesty to

summon to her aid on the supreme occasion the coolness and courage of which she has given such frequent proofs at other times."

The two prisoners were astounded at the boldness of this plan: at first they looked at one another in consternation, for success seemed impossible. They none the less made trial of their disguise: as George had said, it fitted each of them as if they had been measured for it.

Every evening the queen questioned the light, as George had urged, and that for a whole long month, during which each evening the queen and Mary Seyton, although the light gave no fresh tidings, arrayed themselves in their men's clothes, as had been arranged, so that they both acquired such practice that they became as familiar to them as those of their own sex.

At last, the 2nd May, 1568, the queen was awakened by the blowing of a horn: uneasy as to what it announced, she slipped on a cloak and ran to the window, where Mary Seyton joined her directly. A rather numerous band of horsemen had halted on the side of the lake, displaying the Douglas pennon, and three boats were rowing together and vying with each other to fetch the new arrivals.

This event caused the queen dismay: in her situation the least change in the castle routine was to be feared, for it might upset all the concerted plans. This apprehension redoubled when, on the boats drawing near, the queen recognised in the elder Lord Douglas, the husband of Lady Lochleven, and the father of William and George. The venerable knight, who was Keeper of the Marches in the north, was coming to visit his ancient manor, in which he had not set foot for three years.

It was an event for Lochleven; and, some minutes after the arrival of the boats, Mary Stuart heard the old steward's footsteps mounting the stairs: he came to announce his master's arrival to the queen, and, as it must needs be a time of rejoicing to all the castle inhabitants when its master returned, he came to invite the queen to the dinner in celebration of the event: whether instinctively or from distaste, the queen declined.

All day long the bell and the bugle resounded: Lord Douglas, like a true feudal lord, travelled with the retinue of a prince. One saw nothing but new soldiers and servants passing and repassing beneath the queen's windows: the footmen and horsemen were wearing, moreover, a livery similar to that which the queen and Mary Seyton had received.

Mary awaited the night with impatience. The day before, she had questioned her light, and it had informed her as usual, in reappearing at her eleventh or twelfth heart-beat, that the moment of escape was near; but she greatly feared that Lord Douglas's arrival might have upset everything, and that this evening's signal could only announce a postponement. But hardly had she seen the light shine than she placed her lamp in the window; the other disappeared directly, and Mary Stuart, with terrible anxiety, began to question it. This anxiety increased when she had counted more than fifteen beats.

Then she stopped, cast down, her eyes mechanically fixed on the spot where the light had been. But her astonishment was great when, at the end of a few minutes, she did not see it reappear, and when, half an hour having elapsed, everything remained in darkness. The queen then renewed her signal, but obtained no response: the escape was for the same evening.

The queen and Mary Seyton were so little expecting this issue, that, contrary to their custom, they had not put on their men's clothes that evening. They immediately flew to the queen's bed-chamber, bolted the door behind them, and began to dress.

They had hardly finished their hurried toilette when they heard a key turn in the lock: they immediately blew out the lamp. Light steps approached the door. The two women leaned one against the other; for they both were near falling. Someone tapped gently. The queen asked who was there, and Little Douglas's voice answered in the two first lines of an old ballad—

"Douglas, Douglas, Tender and true."

Mary opened, directly: it was the watchword agreed upon with George Douglas.

The child was without a light. He stretched out his hand and encountered the queen's: in the starlight, Mary Stuart saw him kneel down; then she felt the imprint of his lips on her fingers.

"Is your Majesty ready to follow me?" he asked in a low tone, rising.

"Yes, my child," the queen answered: "it is for this evening, then?"

"With your Majesty's permission, yes, it is for this evening."

"Is everything ready?"

"Everything."

"What are we to do?"

"Follow me everywhere."

"My God! my God!" cried Mary Stuart, "have pity on us!" Then, having breathed a short prayer in a low voice, while Mary Seyton was taking the casket in which were the queen's jewels, "I am ready," said she: "and you, darling?"

"I also," replied Mary Seyton.

"Come, then," said Little Douglas.

The two prisoners followed the child; the queen going first, and Mary Seyton after. Their youthful guide carefully shut again the door behind him, so that if a warder happened to pass he would see nothing; then he began to descend the winding stair. Half-way down, the noise of the feast reached them, a mingling of shouts of laughter, the confusion of voices, and the clinking of glasses. The queen placed her hand on her young guide's shoulder.

"Where are you leading us?" she asked him with terror.

"Out of the castle," replied the child.

"But we shall have to pass through the great hall?"

"Without a doubt; and that is exactly what George foresaw. Among the footmen, whose livery your Majesty is wearing, no one will recognise you."

"My God! my God!" the queen murmured, leaning

against the wall.

"Courage, madam," said Mary Seyton in a low voice, "or we are lost."

"You are right," returned the queen; "let us go". And they started again still led by their guide.

At the foot of the stair he stopped, and giving the queen a stone pitcher full of wine—

"Set this jug on your right shoulder, madam," said he; "it will hide your face from the guests, and your Majesty will give rise to less suspicion if carrying something. You, Miss Mary, give me that casket, and put on your head this basket of bread. Now, that's right: do you feel you have strength?"

"Yes," said the queen.

"Yes," said Mary Seyton.

"Then follow me."

The child went on his way, and after a few steps the fugitives found themselves in a kind of antechamber to the great hall, from which proceeded noise and light. Several servants were occupied there with different duties; not one paid attention to them, and that a little reassured the queen. Besides, there was no longer any drawing back: Little Douglas had just entered the great hall.

The guests, seated on both sides of a long table ranged according to the rank of those assembled at it, were beginning dessert, and consequently had reached the gayest moment of the repast. Moreover, the hall was so large that the lamps and candles which lighted it, multiplied as they were, left in the most favourable half-light both sides of the apartment, in which fifteen or twenty servants were coming and going. The queen and Mary Seyton mingled with this crowd, which was too much occupied to notice them, and without stopping, without slackening, without looking back, they crossed the whole length of the hall, reached the other door, and found themselves in the vestibule corresponding to the one they had passed through on coming in. The queen set down her jug there, Mary Seyton her basket, and both, still led by the child, entered a corridor at the end of which they found themselves in the courtyard. A patrol was passing at the moment, but he took no notice of them.

The child made his way towards the garden, still followed by the two women. There, for no little while, it was necessary to try which of all the keys opened the door; it—was a time of inexpressible anxiety. At last the key turned in the lock, the door opened; the queen and Mary Seyton rushed into the garden. The child closed the door behind them.

About two-thirds of the way across, Little Douglas held out his hand as a sign to them to stop; then, putting down the casket and the keys on the ground, he placed his hands together, and blowing into them, thrice imitated the owl's cry so well that it was impossible to believe that a human voice was uttering the sounds; then, picking up the casket and the keys, he kept on his way on tiptoe and with an attentive ear. On getting near the wall, they again stopped, and after a moment's anxious waiting they heard a groan, then something like the sound of a falling body. Some seconds later the owl's cry was—answered by a tu-whit-tu-whoo.

"It is over," Little Douglas said calmly; "come."

"What is over?" asked the queen; "and what is that groan we heard?"

"There was a sentry at the door on to the lake," the child answered, "but he is no longer there."

The queen felt her heart's blood grow cold, at the same tine that a chilly sweat broke out to the roots of her hair; for she perfectly understood: an unfortunate being had just lost his life on her account. Tottering, she leaned on Mary Seyton, who herself felt her strength giving way. Meanwhile Little Douglas was trying the keys: the second opened the door.

"And the queen?" said in a low voice a man who was waiting on the other side of the wall.

"She is following me," replied the child.

George Douglas, for it was he, sprang into the garden, and, taking the queen's arm on one side and Mary Seyton's on the other, he hurried them away quickly to the lake-side. When passing through the doorway Mary Stuart could not help throwing an uneasy look about her, and it seemed to her that a shapeless object was lying at the bottom of the wall, and as she was shuddering all over.

"Do not pity him," said George in a low voice, "for it is a judgment from heaven. That man was the infamous Warden who betrayed us."

"Alas!" said the queen, "guilty as he was, he is none the less dead on my account."

"When it concerned your safety, madam, was one to

haggle over drops of that base blood? But silence! This way, William, this way; let us keep along the wall, whose shadow hides us. The boat is within twenty steps, and we are saved."

With these words, George hurried on the two women still more quickly, and all four, without having been detected, reached the banks of the lake. 'As Douglas had said, a little boat was waiting; and, on seeing the fugitives approach, four rowers, couched along its bottom, rose, and one of them, springing to land, pulled the chain, so that the queen and Mary Seyton could get in. Douglas seated them at the prow, the child placed himself at the rudder, and George, with a kick, pushed off the boat, which began to glide over the lake.

"And now," said he, "we are really saved; for they might as well pursue a sea swallow on Solway Firth as try to reach us. Row, children, row; never mind if they hear us: the main thing is to get into the open."

"Who goes there?" cried a voice above, from the castle terrace.

"Row, row," said Douglas, placing himself in front of the queen.

"The boat! the boat!" cried the same voice; "bring to the boat!" Then, seeing that it continued to recede, "Treason! treason!" cried the sentinel. "To arms!"

At the same moment a flash lit up the lake; the report of a firearm was heard, and a ball passed, whistling. The queen uttered a little cry, although she had run no danger, George, as we have said, having placed himself in front of her, quite protecting her with his body.

The alarm bell now rang, and all the castle lights were seen moving and glancing about, as if distracted, in the rooms.

"Courage, children!" said Douglas. "Row as if your lives depended on each stroke of the oar; for ere five minutes the skiff will be out after us."

"That won't be so easy for them as you think, George," said Little Douglas; "for I shut all the doors behind me, and some time will elapse before the keys that I have left there open them. As to these," added he, showing those he had so skilfully abstracted, "I resign them to the Kelpie, the genie of the lake, and I nominate him porter of Lochleven Castle."

The discharge of a small piece of artillery answered William's joke; but as the night was too dark for one to aim to such a distance as that already between the castle and the boat, the ball ricochetted at twenty paces from the fugitives, while the report died away in echo after echo. Then Douglas drew his pistol from his belt, and, warning the ladies to have no fear, he fired in the air, not to answer by idle bravado the castle cannonade, but to give notice to a troop of faithful friends, who were waiting for them on the other shore of the lake, that the queen had escaped. Immediately, in spite of the danger of being so near Kinross, cries of joy resounded on the bank, and William having turned the rudder, the boat made for land at the spot whence they had been heard. Douglas then gave his hand to the queen, who sprang lightly ashore, and who, falling on her knees, immediately began to give thanks to God for her happy deliverance.

On rising, the queen found herself surrounded by her most faithful servants—Hamilton, Herries, and Seyton, Mary's father. Light-headed with joy, the queen extended her hands to them, thanking them with broken words, which expressed her intoxication and her gratitude better than the choicest phrases could have done, when suddenly, turning round, she perceived George Douglas, alone and melancholy. Then, going to him and taking him by the hand—

"My lords," said she, presenting George to them, and pointing to William, "behold my two deliverers: behold those to whom, as long as I live, I shall preserve gratitude of which nothing will ever acquit me."

"Madam," said Douglas, "each of us has only done what he ought, and he who has risked most is the happiest. But if your Majesty will believe me, you will not lose a moment in needless words."

"Douglas is right," said Lord Seyton. "To horse! to horse!"

Immediately, and while four couriers set out in four different directions to announce to the queen's friends her happy escape, they brought her a horse saddled for her, which she mounted with her usual skill; then the little troop, which, composed of about twenty persons, was escorting the future destiny of Scotland, keeping away from the village of Kinross, to which the castle firing had doubtless given the alarm, took at a gallop the road to Seyton's castle, where was already a garrison large enough to defend the queen from a sudden attack.

The queen journeyed all night, accompanied on one side

by Douglas, on the other by Lord Seyton; then, at daybreak, they stopped at the gate of the castle of West Niddrie, belonging to Lord Seyton, as we have said, and situated in West Lothian. Douglas sprang from his horse to offer his hand to Mary Stuart; but Lord Seyton claimed his privilege as master of the house. The queen consoled Douglas with a glance, and entered the fortress.

"Madam," said Lord Seyton, leading her into a room prepared for her for nine months, "your Majesty must have need of repose, after the fatigue and the emotions you have gone through since yesterday morning; you may sleep here in peace, and disquiet yourself for nothing: any noise you may hear will be made by a reinforcement of friends which we are expecting. As to our enemies, your Majesty has nothing to fear from them so long as you inhabit the castle of a Seyton."

The queen again thanked all her deliverers, gave her hand to Douglas to kiss one last time, kissed Little William on the forehead, and named him her favourite page for the future; then, profiting by the advice given her, entered her room where Mary Seyton, to the exclusion of every other woman, claimed the privilege of performing about her the duties with which she had been charged during their eleven months' captivity in Lochleven Castle.

On opening her eyes, Mary Stuart thought she had had one of those dreams so gainful to prisoners, when waking they see again the bolts on their doors and the bars on their windows. So the queen, unable to believe the evidence of her senses, ran, half dressed, to the window. The courtyard was filled with soldiers, and these soldiers all friends who had hastened at the news of her escape; she recognised the banners of her faithful friends, the Seytons, the Arbroaths, the Herries, and the Hamiltons, and scarcely had she been seen at the window than all these banners bent before her, with the shouts a hundred times repeated of "Long live Mary of Scotland! Long live our queen!" Then, without giving heed to the disarray of her toilet, lovely and chaste with her emotion and her happiness, she greeted them in her turn, her eyes full of tears; but this time they were tears of joy. However, the queen recollected that she was barely covered, and blushing at having allowed herself to be thus carried away in her ecstasy, she abruptly drew back, quite rosy with confusion.

Then she had an instant's womanly fright: she had fled from Lochleven Castle in the Douglas livery, and without either the leisure or the opportunity for taking women's clothes with her. But she could not remain attired as a man; so she explained her uneasiness to Mary Seyton, who responded by opening the closets in the queen's room. They were furnished, not only with robes, the measure for which, like that of the suit, had been taken from Mary Fleming, but also with all the necessaries for a woman's toilet. The queen was astonished: it was like being in a fairy castle.

"Mignonne," said she, looking one after another at the robes, all the stuffs of which were chosen with exquisite taste, "I knew your father was a brave and loyal knight, but I did not think him so learned in the matter of the toilet. We shall name him groom of the wardrobe."

"Alas! madam," smilingly replied Mary Seyton, "you are not mistaken: my father has had everything in the castle furbished up to the last corselet, sharpened to the last sword, unfurled to the last banner; but my father, ready as he is to die for your Majesty, would not have dreamed for an instant of offering you anything but his roof to rest under, or his cloak to cover you. It is Douglas again who has foreseen everything, prepared everything—everything even to Rosabelle, your Majesty's favourite steed, which is impatiently awaiting in the stable the moment when, mounted on her, your Majesty will make your triumphal re-entry into Edinburgh."

"And how has he been able to get her back again?" Mary asked. "I thought that in the division of my spoils Rosabelle had fallen to the fair Alice, my brother's favourite sultana?"

"Yes, yes," said Mary Seyton, "it was so; and as her value was known, she was kept under lock and key by an army of grooms; but Douglas is the man of miracles, and, as I have told you, Rosabelle awaits your Majesty."

"Noble Douglas!" murmured the queen, with eyes full of tears; then, as if speaking to herself, "And this is precisely one of those devotions that we can never repay. The others will be happy with honours, places, money; but to Douglas what matter all these things?"

"Come, madam, come," said Mary Seyton, "God takes on Himself the debts of kings; He will reward Douglas. As to your Majesty, reflect that they are waiting dinner for you. I hope," added she, smiling, "that you will not affront my father as you did Lord Douglas yesterday in refusing to partake of his feast on his fortunate home-coming."

"And luck has come to me for it, I hope," replied Mary. "But you are right, darling: no more sad thoughts; we will consider when we have indeed become queen again what we can do for Douglas."

The queen dressed and went down. As Mary Seyton had told her, the chief noblemen of her party, already gathered round her, were waiting for her in the great hall of the castle. Her arrival was greeted with acclamations of the liveliest enthusiasm, and she sat down to table, with Lord Seyton on her right hand, Douglas on her left, and behind her Little William, who the same day was beginning his duties as page.

Next morning the queen was awakened by the sound of trumpets and bugles: it had been decided the day before that she should set out that day for Hamilton, where reinforcements were looked for. The queen donned an elegant riding-habit, and soon, mounted on Rosabelle, appeared amid her defenders. The shouts of joy redoubled: her beauty, her grace, and her courage were admired by everyone. Mary Stuart became her own self once more, and she felt spring up in her again the power of fascination she had always exercised on those who came near her. Everyone was in good humour, and the happiest of all was perhaps Little William, who for the first time in his life had such a fine dress and such a fine horse.

Two or three thousand men were awaiting the queen at Hamilton, which she reached the same evening; and during the night following her arrival the troops increased to six thousand. The 2nd of May she was a prisoner, without another friend but a child in her prison, without other means of communication with her adherents than the flickering and uncertain light of a lamp, and three days afterwards—that is to say, between the Sunday and the Wednesday—she found herself not only free, but also at the head of a powerful confederacy, which counted at its head nine earls, eight peers, nine bishops, and a number of barons and nobles renowned among the bravest of Scotland.

The advice of the most judicious among those about the queen was to shut herself up in the strong castle of Dumbarton, which, being impregnable, would give all her adherents time to assemble together, distant and scattered as they were: accordingly, the guidance of the troops who were to conduct the queen to that town was entrusted to the Earl of Argyll, and the 11th of May she took the road with an army of nearly ten thousand men.

Murray was at Glasgow when he heard of the queen's escape: the place was strong; he decided to hold it, and summoned to him his bravest and most devoted partisans. Kirkcaldy of Grange, Morton, Lindsay of Byres, Lord Lochleven, and William Douglas hastened to him, and six thousand of the best troops in the kingdom gathered round them, while Lord Ruthven in the counties of Berwick and Angus raised levies with which to join them.

The 13th May, Morton occupied from daybreak the village of Langside, through which the queen must pass to get to Dumbarton. The news of the occupation reached the queen as the two armies were yet seven miles apart. Mary's first instinct was to escape an engagement: she remembered her last battle at Carberry Hill, at the end of which she had been separated from Bothwell and brought to Edinburgh; so she expressed aloud this opinion, which was supported by George Douglas, who, in black armour, without other arms, had continued at the queen's side.

"Avoid an engagement!" cried Lord Seyton, not daring to answer his sovereign, and replying to George as if this opinion had originated with him. "We could do it, perhaps, if we were one to ten; but we shall certainly not do so when we are three to two. You speak a strange tongue, my young master," continued he, with some contempt; "and you forget, it seems to me, that you are a Douglas and that you speak to a Seyton."

"My lord," returned George calmly, "when we only hazard the lives of Douglases and Seytons, you will find me, I hope, as ready to fight as you, be it one to ten, be it three to two; but we are now answerable for an existence dearer to Scotland than that of all the Seytons and all the Douglases. My advice is then to avoid battle."

"Battle! battle!" cried all the chieftains.

"You hear, madam?" said Lord Seyton to Mary Stuart: "I believe that to wish to act against such unanimity would be dangerous. In Scotland, madam, there is an ancient proverb which has it that 'there is most prudence in courage.'"

"But have you not heard that the regent has taken up an

advantageous position?" the queen said.

"The greyhound hunts the hare on the hillside as well as in the plain," replied Seyton: "we will drive him out, wherever he is."

"Let it be as you desire, then, my lords. It shall not be said that Mary Stuart returned to the scabbard the sword her defenders had drawn for her."

Then, turning round to Douglas

"George," she said to him, "choose a guard of twenty men for me, and take command of them: you will not quit me."

George bent low in obedience, chose twenty from among the bravest men, placed the queen in their midst, and put himself at their head; then the troops, which had halted, received the order to continue their road. In two hours' time the advance guard was in sight of the enemy; it halted, and the rest of the army rejoined it.

The queen's troops then found themselves parallel with the city of Glasgow, and the heights which rose in front of them were already occupied by a force above which floated, as above that of Mary, the royal banners of Scotland, On the other side, and on the opposite slope, stretched the village of Langside, encircled with enclosures and gardens. The road which led to it, and which followed all the variations of the ground, narrowed at one place in such a way that two men could hardly pass abreast, then, farther on, lost itself in a ravine, beyond which it reappeared, then branched into two, of which one climbed to the village of Langside, while the other led to Glasgow.

On seeing the lie of the ground, the Earl of Argyll immediately comprehended the importance of occupying this village, and, turning to Lord Seyton, he ordered him to gallop off and try to arrive there before the enemy, who doubtless, having made the same observation as the commander of the royal forces, was setting in motion at that very moment a considerable body of cavalry.

Lord Seyton called up his men directly, but while he was ranging them round his banner, Lord Arbroath drew his sword, and approaching the Earl of Argyll—

"My lord," said he, "you do me a wrong in charging Lord Seyton to seize that post: as commander of the vanguard, it is to me this honour belongs. Allow me, then, to use my privilege in claiming it."

"It is I who received the order to seize it; I will seize it!" cried Seyton.

"Perhaps," returned Lord Arbroath, "but not before me!"

"Before you and before every Hamilton in the world!" exclaimed Seyton, putting his horse to the gallop and rushing down into the hollow road—

"Saint Bennet! and forward!"

"Come, my faithful kinsmen!" cried Lord Arbroath, dashing forward on his side with the same object; "come, my men-at-arms! For God and the queen!"

The two troops precipitated themselves immediately in disorder and ran against one another in the narrow way, where, as we have said, two men could hardly pass abreast. There was a terrible collision there, and the conflict began among friends who should have been united against the enemy. Finally, the two troops, leaving behind them some corpses stifled in the press, or even killed by their companions, passed through the defile pell-mell and were lost sight of in the ravine. But during this struggle Seyton and Arbroath had lost precious time, and the detachment sent by Murray, which had taken the road by Glasgow, had reached the village beforehand; it was now necessary not to take it, but to retake it.

Argyll saw that the whole day's struggle would be concentrated there, and, understanding more and more the importance of the village, immediately put himself at the head of the body of his army, commanding a rearguard of two thousand men to remain there and await further orders to take part in the fighting. But whether the captain who commanded them had ill understood, or whether he was eager to distinguish himself in the eyes of the queen, scarcely had Argyll vanished into the ravine, at the end of which the struggle had already commenced between Kirkcaldy of Grange and Morton on the one side, and on the other between Arbroath and Seyton, than, without regarding the cries of Mary Stuart, he set off in his turn at a gallop, leaving the queen without other guard than the little escort of twenty men which Douglas had chosen for her. Douglas sighed.

"Alas!" said the queen, hearing him, "I am not a soldier, but there it seems to me is a battle very badly begun."

"What is to be done?" replied Douglas. "We are every one of us infatuated, from first to last, and all these men are behaving to-day like madmen or children."

"Victory! victory!" said the queen; "the enemy is retreating, fighting. I see the banners of Seyton and Arbroath floating near the first houses in the village. Oh! my brave lords," cried she, clapping her hands. "Victory! victory!"

But she stopped suddenly on perceiving a body of the enemy's army advancing to charge the victors in flank.

"It is nothing, it is nothing," said Douglas; "so long as there is only cavalry we have nothing much to fear, and besides the Earl of Argyll will fall in in time to aid them."

"George," said Little William.

"Well?" asked Douglas.

"Don't you see?" the child went on, stretching out his arms towards the enemy's force, which was coming on at a gallop.

"What?"

"Each horseman carries a footman armed with an arquebuse behind him, so that the troop is twice as numerous as it appears."

"That's true; upon my soul, the child has good sight. Let someone go at once full gallop and take news of this to the Earl or Argyll."

"I! I!" cried Little William. "I saw them first; it is my right to bear the tidings."

"Go, then, my child," said Douglas; "and may God preserve thee!"

The child flew, quick as lightning, not hearing or feigning not to hear the queen, who was recalling him. He was seen to cross the gorge and plunge into the hollow road at the moment when Argyll was debouching at the end and coming to the aid of Seyton and Arbroath. Meanwhile, the enemy's detachment had dismounted its infantry, which, immediately formed up, was scattering on the sides of the ravine by paths impracticable for horses.

"William will come too late!" cried Douglas, "or even, should he arrive in time, the news is now useless to them. Oh madmen, madmen that we are! This is how we have always lost all our battles!"

"Is the battle lost, then?" demanded Mary, growing pale.

"No, madam, no," cried Douglas; "Heaven be thanked, not yet; but through too great haste we have begun badly."

"And William?" said Mary Stuart.

"He is now serving his apprenticeship in arms; for, if I am not mistaken, he must be at this moment at the very spot where those marksmen are making such quick firing."

"Poor child!" cried the queen; "if ill should befall him, I shall never console myself."

"Alas! madam," replied Douglas, "I greatly fear that his first battle is his last, and that everything is already over for him; for, unless I mistake, there is his horse returning riderless."

"Oh, my God! my God!" said the queen, weeping, and raising her hands to heaven, "it is then decreed that I should be fatal to all around me!"

George was not deceived: it was William's horse coming back without his young master and covered with blood.

"Madam," said Douglas, "we are ill placed here; let us

gain that hillock on which is the Castle of Crookstone: from thence we shall survey the whole battlefield."

"No, not there! not there!" said the queen in terror: "within that castle I came to spend the first days of my marriage with Darnley; it will bring me misfortune."

"Well, beneath that yew-tree, then," said George, pointing to another slight rise near the first; "but it is important for us to lose no detail of this engagement. Everything depends perhaps for your Majesty on an ill-judged manoeuvre or a lost moment."

"Guide me, then," the queen said; "for, as for me, I no longer see it. Each report of that terrible cannonade echoes to the depths of my heart."

However well placed as was this eminence for overlooking from its summit the whole battlefield, the reiterated discharge of cannon and musketry covered it with such a cloud of smoke that it was impossible to make out from it anything but masses lost amid a murderous fog. At last, when an hour had passed in this desperate conflict, through the skirts of this sea of smoke the fugitives were seen to emerge and disperse in all directions, followed by the victors. Only, at that distance, it was impossible to make out who had gained or lost the battle, and the banners, which on both sides displayed the Scottish arms, could in no way clear up this confusion.

At that moment there was seen coming down from the Glasgow hillsides all the remaining reserve of Murray's army; it was coming at full speed to engage in the fighting;

but this manoeuvre might equally well have for its object the support of defeated friends as to complete the rout of the enemy. However, soon there was no longer any doubt; for this reserve charged the fugitives, amid whom it spread fresh confusion. The queen's army was beaten. At the same time, three or four horsemen appeared on the hither side of the ravine, advancing at a gallop. Douglas recognised them as enemies.

"Fly, madam," cried George, "fly without loss of a second; for those who are coming upon us are followed by others. Gain the road, while I go to check them. And you," added he, addressing the escort, "be killed to the last man rather than let them take your queen."

"George! George!" cried the queen, motionless, and as if riveted to the spot.

But George had already dashed away with all his horse's speed, and as he was splendidly mounted, he flew across the space with lightning rapidity, and reached the gorge before the enemy. There he stopped, put his lance in rest, and alone against five bravely awaited the encounter.

As to the queen, she had no desire to go; but, on the contrary, as if turned to stone, she remained in the same place, her eyes fastened on this combat which was taking place at scarcely five hundred paces from her. Suddenly, glancing at her enemies, she saw that one of them bore in the middle of his shield a bleeding heart, the Douglas arms. Then she uttered a cry of pain, and drooping her head—

"Douglas against Douglas; brother against brother!" she

murmured: "it only wanted this last blow."

"Madam, madam," cried her escort, "there is not an instant to lose: the young master of Douglas cannot hold out long thus alone against five; let us fly! let us fly!" And two of them taking the queen's horse by the bridle, put it to the gallop, at the moment when George, after having beaten down two of his enemies and wounded a third, was thrown down in his turn in the dust, thrust to the heart by a lance-head. The queen groaned on seeing him fall; then, as if he alone had detained her, and as if he being killed she had no interest in anything else, she put Rosabelle to the gallop, and as she and her troop were splendidly mounted, they had soon lost sight of the battlefield.

She fled thus for sixty miles, without taking any rest, and without ceasing to weep or to sigh: at last, having traversed the counties of Renfrew and Ayr, she reached the Abbey of Dundrennan, in Galloway, and certain of being, for the time at least, sheltered from every danger, she gave the order to stop. The prior respectfully received her at the gate of the convent.

"I bring you misfortune and ruin, father," said the queen, alighting from her horse.

"They are welcome," replied the prior, "since they come accompanied by duty."

The queen gave Rosabelle to the care of one of the men-at-arms who had accompanied her, and leaning on Mary Seyton, who had not left her for a moment, and on Lord Herries, who had rejoined her on the road, she entered the convent.

Lord Herries had not concealed her position from Mary Stuart: the day had been completely lost, and with the day, at least for the present, all hope of reascending the throne of Scotland. There remained but three courses for the queen to take to withdraw into France, Spain or England. On the advice of Lord Herries, which accorded with her own feeling, she decided upon the last; and that same night she wrote this double missive in verse and in prose to Elizabeth:

"MY DEAR SISTER,—I have often enough begged you to receive my tempest-tossed vessel into your haven during the storm. If at this pass she finds a safe harbour there, I shall cast anchor there for ever: otherwise the bark is in God's keeping, for she is ready and caulked for defence on her voyage against all storms. I have dealt openly with you, and still do so: do not take it in bad part if I write thus; it is not in defiance of you, as it appears, for in everything I rely on your friendship."

"This sonnet accompanied the letter:—

"One thought alone brings danger and delight; Bitter and sweet change places in my heart, With doubt, and then with hope, it takes its part, Till peace and rest alike are put to flight.

Therefore, dear sister, if this card pursue That keen desire by which I am oppressed, To see you, 'tis because I live distressed, Unless some swift and sweet result ensue.

Beheld I have my ship compelled by fate To seek the open sea, when close to port, And calmest days break into storm and gale; Wherefore full grieved and fearful is my state, Not for your sake, but since, in evil sort, Fortune so oft snaps strongest rope and sail."

Elizabeth trembled with joy at receiving this double letter; for the eight years that her enmity had been daily increasing to Mary Stuart, she had followed her with her eyes continually, as a wolf might a gazelle; at last the gazelle sought refuge in the wolf's den. Elizabeth had never hoped as much: she immediately despatched an order to the Sheriff of Cumberland to make known to Mary that she was ready to receive her. One morning a bugle was heard blowing on the sea-shore: it was Queen Elizabeth's envoy come to fetch Queen Mary Stuart.

Then arose great entreaties to the fugitive not to trust herself thus to a rival in power, glory, and beauty; but the poor dispossessed queen was full of confidence in her she called her good sister, and believed herself going, free and rid of care, to take at Elizabeth's court the place due to her rank and her misfortunes: thus she persisted, in spite of all that could be said. In our time, we have seen the same infatuation seize another royal fugitive, who like Mary Stuart confided himself to the generosity of his enemy England: like Mary Stuart, he was cruelly punished for his confidence, and found in the deadly climate of St. Helena the scaffold of Fotheringay.

Mary Stuart set out on her journey, then, with her little following. Arrived at the shore of Solway Firth, she found there the Warden of the English Marches: he was a gentleman named Lowther, who received the queen with the greatest respect, but who gave her to understand that he could not permit more than three of her women to accompany her. Mary Seyton immediately claimed her privilege: the queen held out to her her hand.

"Alas! mignonne," said she, "but it might well be another's turn: you have already suffered enough for me and with me."

But Mary, unable to reply, clung to her hand, making a sign with her head that nothing in the world should part her from her mistress. Then all who had accompanied the queen renewed their entreaties that she should not persist in this fatal resolve, and when she was already a third of the way along the plank placed for her to enter the skiff, the Prior of Dundrennan, who had offered Mary Stuart such dangerous and touching hospitality, entered the water up to his knees, to try to detain her; but all was useless: the queen had made up her mind.

At that, moment Lowther approached her. "Madam," said he, "accept anew my regrets that I cannot offer a warm welcome in England to all who would wish to follow you there; but our queen has given us positive orders, and we must carry them out. May I be permitted to remind your Majesty that the tide serves?"

"Positive orders!" cried the prior. "Do you hear, madam? Oh! you are lost if you quit this shore! Back, while there is yet time! Back; madam, in Heaven's name! To me, sir knights, to me!" he cried, turning to Lord Herries and the other lords who had accompanied Mary Stuart; "do not allow your queen to abandon you, were it needful to struggle with her and the English at the same time. Hold her back, my lords, in Heaven's name! withhold her!"

"What means this violence, sir priest?" said the Warden of the Marches. "I came here at your queen's express command; she is free to return to you, and there is no need to have recourse to force for that". Then, addressing the queen—

"Madam," said he, "do you consent to follow me into England in full liberty of choice? Answer, I entreat you; for my honour demands that the whole world should be aware that you have followed me freely."

"Sir," replied Mary Stuart, "I ask your pardon, in the name of this worthy servant of God and his queen, for what he may have said of offence to you. Freely I leave Scotland and place myself in your hands, trusting that I shall be free either to remain in England with my royal sister, or to return to France to my worthy relatives". Then, turning to the priest, "Your blessing, father, and God protect you!"

"Alas! alas!" murmured the abbot, obeying the queen, "it is not we who are in need of God's protection, but rather you, my daughter. May the blessing of a poor priest turn aside from you the misfortunes I foresee! Go, and may it be with you as the Lord has ordained in His wisdom and in His mercy!"

Then the queen gave her hand to the sheriff, who conducted her to the skiff, followed by Mary Seyton and two other women only. The sails were immediately unfurled, and the little vessel began to recede from the shores of Galloway, to make her way towards those of Cumberland. So long as it could be seen, they who had accompanied the queen lingered on the beach, waving her signs of adieu, which, standing on the deck of the shallop which was bearing her, away, she returned with her handkerchief. Finally, the boat disappeared, and all burst into lamentations or into sobbing. They were right, for the good Prior of Dundrennan's presentiments were only too true, and they had seen Mary Stuart for the last time.

CHAPTER VIII

On landing on the shores of England, the Queen of Scotland found messengers from Elizabeth empowered to express to her all the regret their mistress felt in being unable to admit her to her presence, or to give her the affectionate welcome she bore her in her heart. But it was essential, they added, that first of all the queen should clear herself of the death of Darnley, whose family, being subjects of the Queen of England, had a right to her protection and justice.

Mary Stuart was so blinded that she did not see the trap, and immediately offered to prove her innocence to the satisfaction of her sister Elizabeth; but scarcely had she in her hands Mary Stuart's letter, than from arbitress she became judge, and, naming commissioners to hear the parties, summoned Murray to appear and accuse his sister. Murray, who knew Elizabeth's secret intentions with regard to her rival, did not hesitate a moment. He came to England, bringing the casket containing the three letters we have quoted, some verses and some other papers which proved that the queen had not only been Bothwell's mistress during the lifetime of Darnley, but had also been aware of the assassination of her husband. On their side, Lord Herries and the Bishop of Ross, the queen's advocates, maintained that these letters had been forged, that the handwriting was counterfeited, and demanded, in verification, experts whom they could not obtain; so that this great controversy, remained pending for future ages, and to this hour nothing is yet affirmatively settled in this matter either by scholars or historians.

After a five months' inquiry, the Queen of England made known to the parties, that not having, in these proceedings, been able to discover anything to the dishonour of accuser or accused, everything would remain in statu quo till one or the other could bring forward fresh proofs.

As a result of this strange decision, Elizabeth should have sent back the regent to Scotland, and have left Mary Stuart free to go where she would. But, instead of that, she had her prisoner removed from Bolton Castle to Carlisle Castle, from whose terrace, to crown her with grief, poor Mary Stuart saw the blue mountains of her own Scotland.

However, among the judges named by Elizabeth to examine into Mary Stuart's conduct was Thomas Howard, Duke of Norfolk. Be it that he was convinced of Mary's innocence, be it that he was urged by the ambitious project which since served as a ground for his prosecution, and which was nothing else than to wed Mary Stuart, to affiance his daughter to the young king, and to become regent of Scotland, he resolved to extricate her from her prison. Several members of the high nobility of England, among whom were the Earls of Westmoreland and Northumberland, entered into the plot and under, took to support it with all their forces. But their scheme had been communicated to the regent: he denounced it to Elizabeth, who had Norfolk arrested. Warned in time, Westmoreland and Northumberland crossed the frontiers and took refuge in the Scottish borders which were favourable to Queen Mary. The former reached Flanders, where he died in exile; the latter, given up to Murray, was sent to the castle of Lochleven, which guarded him more faithfully than it had done its royal prisoner. As to Norfolk, he was beheaded. As one sees, Mary Stuart's star had lost none of its fatal influence.

Meanwhile the regent had returned to Edinburgh, enriched with presents from Elizabeth, and having gained, in fact, his case with her, since Mary remained a prisoner. He employed himself immediately in dispersing the remainder of her adherents, and had hardly shut the gates of Lochleven Castle upon Westmoreland than, in the name of the young King James VI, he pursued those who had upheld his mother's cause, and among them more particularly the Hamiltons, who since the affair of "sweeping the streets of Edinburgh," had been the mortal enemies of the Douglases personally; six of the chief members of this family were condemned to death, and only obtained commutation of the penalty into an eternal exile on the entreaties of John Knox, at that time so powerful in Scotland that Murray dared not refuse their pardon.

One of the amnestied was a certain Hamilton of Bothwellhaugh, a man of ancient Scottish times, wild and vindictive as the nobles in the time of James I. He had withdrawn into the highlands, where he had found an asylum, when he learned that Murray, who in virtue of the confiscation pronounced against exiles had given his lands to one of his favourites, had had the cruelty to expel his sick and bedridden wife from her own house, and that without giving her time to dress, and although it was in the winter cold. The poor woman, besides, without shelter, without clothes, and without food, had gone out of her mind, had wandered about thus for some time, an object of compassion but equally of dread; for everyone had been afraid of compromising himself by assisting her. At last, she had returned to expire of misery and cold on the threshold whence she had been driven.

On learning this news, Bothwellhaugh, despite the violence of his character, displayed no anger: he merely responded, with a terrible smile, "It is well; I shall avenge her."

Next day, Bothwellhaugh left his highlands, and came down, disguised, into the plain, furnished with an order of admission from the Archbishop of St. Andrews to a house which this prelate—who, as one remembers, had followed the queen's fortunes to the last moment—had at Linlithgow. This house, situated in the main street, had a wooden balcony looking on to the square, and a gate which opened out into the country. Bothwellhaugh entered it at night, installed himself on the first floor, hung black cloth on the walls so that his shadow should not be seen from without, covered the floor with mattresses so that his footsteps might not be heard on the ground floor, fastened a racehorse ready saddled and bridled in the garden, hollowed out the upper part of the little gate which led to the open country so that he could pass through it at a gallop, armed himself with a loaded arquebuse, and shut himself up in the room.

All these preparations had been made, one imagines, because Murray was to spend the following day in Linlithgow. But, secret as they were, they were to be rendered useless, for the regent's friends warned him that it would not be safe for him to pass through the town, which belonged almost wholly to the Hamiltons, and advised him to go by it. However, Murray was courageous, and, accustomed not to give way before a real danger, he did nothing but laugh at a peril which he looked upon as imaginary, and boldly followed his first plan, which was not to go out of his way. Consequently, as the street into which the Archbishop of St. Andrews' balcony looked was on his road, he entered upon it, not going rapidly and preceded by guards who would open up a passage for him, as his friends still counselled, but advancing at a foot's pace, delayed as he was by the great crowd which was blocking up the streets to see him. Arrived in front of the balcony, as if chance had been in tune with the murderer, the crush became so great that Murray was obliged to halt for a moment: this rest gave Bothwellhaugh time to adjust himself for a steady shot. He leaned his arquebuse on the balcony, and, having taken aim with the necessary leisure and coolness, fired. Bothwellhaugh had put such a charge into the arquebuse, that the ball, having passed through the regent's heart, killed the horse of a gentleman on his right. Murray fell directly, saying, "My God! I am killed."

As they had seen from which window the shot was fired, the persons in the regent's train had immediately thrown themselves against the great door of the house which looked on to the street, and had smashed it in; but they only arrived in time to see Bothwellhaugh fly through the little garden gate on the horse he had got ready: they immediately remounted the horses they had left in the street, and, passing through the house, pursued him. Bothwellhaugh had a good horse and the lead of his enemies; and yet, four of them, pistol in hand, were so well mounted that they were beginning to gain upon him. Then Bothwellhaugh; seeing that whip and spur were not enough, drew his dagger and used it to goad on his horse. His horse, under this terrible stimulus, acquired fresh vigour, and, leaping a gully eighteen feet deep, put between his master and his pursuers a barrier which they dared not cross.

The murderer sought an asylum in France, where he retired under the protection of the Guises. There, as the bold stroke he had attempted had acquired him a great reputation, some days before the Massacre of St. Bartholomew, they made him overtures to assassinate Admiral Coligny. But Bothwellhaugh indignantly repulsed these proposals, saying that he was the avenger of abuses and not an assassin, and that those who had to complain of the admiral had only to come and ask him how he had done, and to do as he.

As to Murray, he died the night following his wound, leaving the regency to the Earl of Lennox, the father of Darnley: on learning the news of his death, Elizabeth wrote that she had lost her best friend.

While these events were passing in Scotland, Mary Stuart was still a prisoner, in spite of the pressing and successive protests of Charles IX and Henry III. Taking fright at the attempt made in her favour, Elizabeth even had her removed to Sheffield Castle, round which fresh patrols were incessantly in motion.

But days, months, years passed, and poor Mary, who had borne so impatiently her eleven months' captivity in Lochleven Castle, had been already led from prison to prison for fifteen or sixteen years, in spite of her protests and those of the French and Spanish ambassadors, when she was finally taken to Tutbury Castle and placed under the care of Sir Amyas Paulet, her last gaoler: there she found for her sole lodging two low and damp rooms, where little by little what strength remained to her was so exhausted that there were days on which she could not walk, on account of the pain in all her limbs. Then it was that she who had been the queen of two kingdoms, who was born in a gilded cradle and brought up in silk and velvet, was forced to humble herself to ask of her gaoler a softer bed and warmer coverings. This request, treated as an affair of state, gave rise to negotiations which lasted a month, after which the prisoner was at length granted what she asked. And yet the unhealthiness, cold, and privations of all kinds still did not work actively enough on that healthy and robust organisation. They tried to convey to Paulet what a service he would render the Queen of England in cutting short the existence of her who, already condemned in her rival's mind, yet delayed to die. But Sir Amyas Paulet, coarse and harsh as he was to Mary Stuart, declared that, so long as she was with him she would have nothing to fear from poison or dagger, because he would taste all the dishes served to his prisoner, and that no one should approach her but in his presence. In fact, some assassins, sent by Leicester, the very same who had aspired for a moment to the hand of the lovely Mary Stuart, were driven from the castle directly its stern keeper had learned with what intentions they had entered it. Elizabeth had to be patient, then, in contenting herself with tormenting her whom she could not kill, and still hoping that a fresh opportunity would occur for bringing her to trial. That opportunity, so long delayed, the fatal star of Mary Stuart at length brought.

A young Catholic gentleman, a last scion of that ancient chivalry which was already dying out at that time, excited by the excommunication of Pius V, which pronounced Elizabeth fallen from her kingdom on earth and her salvation in heaven, resolved to restore liberty to Mary, who thenceforth was beginning to be looked upon, no longer as a political prisoner, but as a martyr for her faith. Accordingly, braving the law which Elizabeth had had made in 1585, and which provided that, if any attempt on her person was meditated by, or for, a person who thought he had claims to the crown of England, a commission would be appointed composed of twenty-five members, which, to the exclusion of every other tribunal, would be empowered to examine into the offence, and to condemn the guilty persons, whosoever they might be. Babington, not at all discouraged by the example of his predecessors, assembled five of his friends, Catholics as zealous as himself, who engaged their life and honour in the plot of which he was the head, and which had as its aim to assassinate Elizabeth, and as a result to place Mary Stuart on the English throne. But this scheme, well planned as it was, was revealed to Walsingham, who allowed the conspirators to go as far as he thought he could without danger, and who, the day before that fixed for the assassination, had them arrested.

This imprudent and desperate attempt delighted Elizabeth, for, according to the letter of the law, it finally gave her rival's life into her hands. Orders were immediately given to Sir Amyas Paulet to seize the prisoner's papers and to move her to Fotheringay Castle. The gaoler, then, hypocritically relaxing his usual severity, suggested to Mary Stuart that she should go riding, under the pretext that she had need of an airing. The poor prisoner, who for three years had only seen the country through her prison bars, joyfully accepted, and left Tutbury between two guards, mounted, for greater security, on a horse whose feet were hobbled. These two guards took her to Fotheringay Castle, her new habitation, where she found the apartment she was to lodge in already hung in black. Mary Stuart had entered alive into her tomb. As to Babington and his accomplices, they had been already beheaded.

Meanwhile, her two secretaries, Curle and Nau, were arrested, and all her papers were seized and sent to Elizabeth, who, on her part, ordered the forty commissioners to assemble, and proceed without intermission to the trial of the prisoner. They arrived at Fotheringay the 14th October

1586; and next day, being assembled in the great hall of the castle, they began the examination.

At first Mary refused to appear before them, declaring that she did not recognise the commissioners as judges, they not being her peers, and not acknowledging the English law, which had never afforded her protection, and which had constantly abandoned her to the rule of force. But seeing that they proceeded none the less, and that every calumny was allowed, no one being there to refute it, she resolved to appear before the commissioners. We quote the two interrogatories to which Mary Stuart submitted as they are set down in the report of M. de Bellievre to M. de Villeroy. M. de Bellievre, as we shall see later, had been specially sent by King Henry III to Elizabeth. [Intelligence for M. Villeroy of what was done in England by M. de Bellievre about the affairs of the Queen of Scotland, in the months of November and December 1586 and January 1587.]

The said lady being seated at the end of the table in the said hall, and the said commissioners about her—

The Queen of Scotland began to speak in these terms:

"I do not admit that any one of you here assembled is my peer or my judge to examine me upon any charge. Thus what I do, and now tell you, is of my own free will, taking God to witness that I am innocent and pure in conscience of the accusations and slanders of which they wish to accuse me. For I am a free princess and born a queen, obedient to no one, save to God, to whom alone I must give an account of my actions. This is why I protest yet again that my appearance before you be not prejudicial either to me, or to the kings, princes and potentates, my allies, nor to my son, and I require that my protest be registered, and I demand the record of it."

Then the chancellor, who was one of the commissioners, replied in his turn, and protested against the protestation; then he ordered that there should be read over to the Queen of Scotland the commission in virtue of which they were proceeding—a commission founded on the statutes and law of the kingdom.

But to this Mary Stuart made answer that she again protested; that the said statutes and laws were without force against her, because these statutes and laws are not made for persons of her condition.

To this the chancellor replied that the commission intended to proceed against her, even if she refused to answer, and declared that the trial should proceed; for she was doubly subject to indictment, the conspirators having not only plotted in her favour, but also with her consent: to which the said Queen of Scotland responded that she had never even thought of it.

Upon this, the letters it was alleged she had written to Babington and his answers were read to her.

Mary Stuart then affirmed that she had never seen Babington, that she had never had any conference with him, had never in her life received a single letter from him, and that she defied anyone in the world to maintain that she had ever done anything to the prejudice of the said Queen of England; that besides, strictly guarded as she was, away from all news, withdrawn from and deprived of those nearest her, surrounded with enemies, deprived finally of all advice, she had been unable to participate in or to consent to the practices of which she was accused; that there are, besides, many persons who wrote to her what she had no knowledge of, and that she had received a number of letters without knowing whence they came to her.

Then Babington's confession was read to her; but she replied that she did not know what was meant; that besides, if Babington and his accomplices had said such things, they were base men, false and liars.

"Besides," added she, "show me my handwriting and my signature, since you say that I wrote to Babington, and not copies counterfeited like these which you have filled at your leisure with the falsehoods it has pleased you to insert."

Then she was shown the letter that Babington, it was said, had written her. She glanced at it; then said, "I have no knowledge of this letter". Upon this, she was shown her reply, and she said again, "I have no more knowledge of this answer. If you will show me my own letter and my own signature containing what you say, I will acquiesce in all; but up to the present, as I have already told you, you have produced nothing worthy of credence, unless it be the copies you have invented and added to with what seemed good to you."

With these words, she rose, and with her eyes full of tears—

"If I have ever," said she, "consented to such intrigues,

having for object my sister's death, I pray God that He have neither pity nor mercy on me. I confess that I have written to several persons, that I have implored them to deliver me from my wretched prisons, where I languished, a captive and ill-treated princess, for nineteen years and seven months; but it never occurred to me, even in thought, to write or even to desire such things against the queen. Yes, I also confess to having exerted myself for the deliverance of some persecuted Catholics, and if I had been able, and could yet, with my own blood, protect them and save them from their pains, I would have done it, and would do it for them with all my power, in order to save them from destruction."

Then, turning to the secretary, Walsingham—

"But, my lord," said she, "from the moment I see you here, I know whence comes this blow: you have always been my greatest enemy and my son's, and you have moved everyone against me and to my prejudice."

Thus accused to his face, Walsingham rose.

"Madam," he replied, "I protest before God, who is my witness, that you deceive yourself, and that I have never done anything against you unworthy of a good man, either as an individual or as a public personage."

This is all that was said and done that day in the proceedings, till the next day, when the queen was again obliged to appear before the commissioners.

And, being seated at the end of the table of the said hall, and the said commissioners about her, she began to speak in a loud voice.

"You are not unaware, my lords and gentlemen, that I am a sovereign queen, anointed and consecrated in the church of God, and cannot, and ought not, for any reason whatever, be summoned to your courts, or called to your bar, to be judged by the law and statutes that you lay down; for I am a princess and free, and I do not owe to any prince more than he owes to me; and on everything of which I am accused towards my said sister, I cannot, reply if you do not permit me to be assisted by counsel. And if you go further, do what you will; but from all your procedure, in reiterating my protestations, I appeal to God, who is the only just and true judge, and to the kings and princes, my allies and confederates."

This protestation was once more registered, as she had required of the commissioners. Then she was told that she had further written several letters to the princes of Christendom, against the queen and the kingdom of England.

"As to that," replied Mary Stuart, "it is another matter, and I do not deny it; and if it was again to do, I should do as I have done, to gain my liberty; for there is not a man or woman in the world, of less rank than I, who would not do it, and who would not make use of the help and succour of their friends to issue from a captivity as harsh as mine was. You charge me with certain letters from Babington: well, I do not deny that he has written to me and that I have replied to him; but if you find in my answers a single word about the queen my sister, well, yes, there will be good cause to prosecute me. I replied to him who wrote to me that he would set me at liberty, that I accepted his offer, if he could do it without compromising the one or the other of us: that is all.

"As to my secretaries," added the queen, "not they, but torture spoke by their mouths: and as to the confessions of Babington and his accomplices, there is not much to be made of them; for now that they are dead you can say all that seems good to you; and let who will believe you."

With these words, the queen refused to answer further if she were not given counsel, and, renewing her protestation, she withdrew into her apartment; but, as the chancellor had threatened, the trial was continued despite her absence.

However, M. de Chateauneuf, the French ambassador to London, saw matters too near at hand to be deceived as to their course: accordingly, at the first rumour which came to him of bringing Mary Stuart to trial, he wrote to King Henry III, that he might intervene in the prisoner's favour. Henry III immediately despatched to Queen Elizabeth an embassy extraordinary, of which M. de Bellievre was the chief; and at the same time, having learned that James VI, Mary's son, far from interesting himself in his mother's fate, had replied to the French minister, Courcelles, who spoke to him of her, "I can do nothing; let her drink what she has spilled," he wrote him the following letter, to decide the young prince to second him in the steps he was going to take:

"21st November, 1586.

"COURCELLES, I have received your letter of the 4th October last, in which I have seen the discourse that the King of Scotland has held with you concerning what you have witnessed to him of the good affection I bear him, discourse in which he has given proof of desiring to reciprocate it entirely; but I wish that that letter had informed me also that he was better disposed towards the queen his mother, and that he had the heart and the desire to arrange everything in a way to assist her in the affliction in which she now is, reflecting that the prison where she has been unjustly detained for eighteen years and more has induced her to lend an ear to many things which have been proposed to her for gaining her liberty, a thing which is naturally greatly desired by all men, and more still by those who are born sovereigns and rulers, who bear being kept prisoners thus with less patience. He should also consider that if the Queen of England, my good sister, allows herself to be persuaded by the counsels of those who wish that she should stain herself with Queen Mary's blood, it will be a matter which will bring him to great dishonour, inasmuch as one will judge that he will have refused his mother the good offices that he should render her with the said Queen of England, and which would have perhaps been sufficient to move her, if he would have employed them, as warmly, and as soon as his natural duty commanded him. Moreover, it is to be feared for him, that, his mother dead, his own turn may come, and that one may think of doing as much for him, by some violent means, to make the English succession easier to seize for those who are likely to have it after the said Queen Elizabeth, and not only to defraud the said King of Scotland of the claim he can put forward, but to render doubtful even that which he has to his own crown. I do not know in what condition the affairs of my said sister-in-law will be when you receive this letter; but I will tell you that in every case I wish you to rouse strongly the said King of Scotland, with remonstrances, and everything else which may bear on this subject, to embrace the defence and protection of his said mother, and to express to him, on my part, that as this will be a matter for which he will be greatly praised by all the other kings and sovereign princes, he must be assured that if he fails in it there will be great censure for him, and perhaps notable injury to himself in particular. Furthermore, as to the state of my own affairs, you know that the queen, madam and mother, is about to see very soon the King of Navarre, and to confer with him on the matter of the pacification of the troubles of this kingdom, to which, if he bear as much good affection as I do for my part, I hope that things may come to a good conclusion, and that my subjects will have some respite from the great evils and calamities that the war occasions them: supplicating the Creator, Courcelles, that He may have you in His holy keeping.

"Written at St. Germain-en-Laye, the 21st day of November 1586.(Signed) HENRI,

"And below, BRULART."

This letter finally decided James VI to make a kind of demonstration in his mother's favour: he sent Gray, Robert Melville, and Keith to Queen Elizabeth. But although London was nearer Edinburgh than was Paris, the French envoys reached it before the Scotch.

It is true that on reaching Calais, the 27th of November, M. de Bellievre had found a special messenger there to tell him not to lose an instant, from M. de Chateauneuf, who, to provide for every difficulty, had chartered a vessel ready in the harbour. But however great the speed these noble lords wished to make, they were obliged to await the wind's goodwill, which did not allow them to put to sea till Friday 28th at midnight; next day also, on reaching Dover at nine o'clock, they were so shaken by sea-sickness that they were forced to stay a whole day in the town to recover, so that it was not till Sunday 30th that M. de Bellievre was able to set out in the coach that M. Chateauneuf sent him by M. de Brancaleon, and take the road to London, accompanied by the gentlemen of his suite, who rode on post-horses; but resting only a few hours on the way to make up for lost time, they at last arrived in London, Sunday the 1st of December at midday. M. de Bellievre immediately sent one of the gentlemen of his suite, named M. de Villiers, to the Queen of England, who was holding her court at Richmond Castle: the decree had been secretly pronounced already six days, and submitted to Parliament, which was to deliberate upon it with closed doors.

The French ambassadors could not have chosen a worse moment to approach Elizabeth; and to gain time she declined to receive M. de Villiers, returning the answer that he would himself know next day the reason for this refusal. And indeed, next day, the rumour spread in London that the French Embassy had contagion, and that two of the lords in it having died of the plague at Calais, the queen, whatever wish she might have to be agreeable to Henry III, could not endanger her precious existence by receiving his envoys. Great was the astonishment of M. de Bellievre at learning this news he protested that the queen was led into error by a false report, and insisted on being received. Nevertheless, the delays lasted another six days; but as the ambassadors threatened to depart without waiting longer, and as, upon the whole, Elizabeth, disquieted by Spain, had no desire to embroil herself with France, she had M. de Bellievre informed on the morning of the 7th of December that she was ready to receive him after dinner at Richmond Castle, together with the noblemen of his suite.

At the appointed time the French ambassadors presented themselves at the castle gates, and, having been brought to the queen, found her seated on her throne and surrounded by the greatest lords in her kingdom. Then MM. de Chateauneuf and de Bellievre, the one the ambassador in ordinary and the other the envoy extraordinary, having greeted her on the part of the King of France, began to make her the remonstrances with which they were charged. Elizabeth replied, not only in the same French tongue, but also in the most beautiful speech in use at that time, and, carried away by passion, pointed out to the envoys of her brother Henry that the Queen of Scotland had always proceeded against her, and that this was the third time that she had wished to attempt her life by an infinity of ways; which she had already borne too long and with too much patience, but that never had anything so profoundly cut her to the heart as her last conspiracy; that event, added she with sadness, having caused her to sigh more and to shed more tears than the loss of all her relations, so much the more that the Queen of Scotland was her near relative and closely connected with the King of France; and as, in their remonstrances, MM. de Chateauneuf and de Bellievre had brought forward several examples drawn from history, she assumed, in reply to them on this occasion, the pedantic style which was usual with her, and told them that she had seen and read a great many books in her life, and a thousand more than others of her sex and her rank were wont to, but that she had never found in them a single example of a deed like that attempted on her—a deed pursued by a relative, whom the king her brother could not and ought not to support in her wickedness, when it was, on the contrary, his duty to hasten the just punishment of it: then she added, addressing herself specially to M. de Bellievre, and coming down again from the height of her pride to a gracious countenance, that she greatly regretted he was not deputed for a better occasion; that in a few days she would reply to King Henry her brother, concerning whose health she was solicitous, as well as that of the queen mother, who must experience such great fatigue from the trouble she took to restore peace to her son's kingdom; and then, not wishing to hear more, she withdrew into her room.

The envoys returned to London, where they awaited the promised reply; but while they were expecting it unavailingly, they heard quietly the sentence of death given against Queen Mary, which decided them to return to Richmond to make fresh remonstrances to Queen Elizabeth. After two or three fruitless journeys, they were at last, December 15th, admitted for the second time to the royal presence.

The queen did not deny that the sentence had been pronounced, and as it was easy to see that she did not intend in this case to use her right of pardon, M. de Bellievre, judging that there was nothing to be done, asked for a safe-conduct to return to his king: Elizabeth promised it to him within two or three days.

On the following Tuesday, the 17th of the same month of December, Parliament as well as the chief lords of the realm were convoked at the Palace of Westminster, and there, in full court and before all, sentence of death was proclaimed and pronounced against Mary Stuart: then this same sentence, with great display and great solemnity, was read in the squares and at the cross-roads of London, whence it spread throughout the kingdom; and upon this proclamation the bells rang for twenty-four hours, while the strictest orders were given to each of the inhabitants to light bonfires in front of their houses, as is the custom in France on the Eve of St. John the Baptist.

Then, amid this sound of bells, by the light of these bonfires, M. de Bellievre, wishing to make a last effort, in order to have nothing with which to reproach himself, wrote the following letter to Queen Elizabeth:

"MADAM:—We quitted your Majesty yesterday, expecting, as it had pleased you to inform us, to receive in a few days your reply touching the prayer that we made you on behalf of our good master, your brother, for the Queen

Mary Stuart

of Scotland, his sister in-law and confederate; but as this morning we have been informed that the judgment given against the said queen has been proclaimed in London, although we had promised ourselves another issue from your clemency and the friendship your bear to the said lord king your good brother, nevertheless, to neglect no part of our duty, and believing in so doing to serve the intentions of the king our master, we have not wanted to fail to write to you this present letter, in which we supplicate you once again, very humbly, not to refuse his Majesty the very pressing and very affectionate prayer that he has made you, that you will be pleased to preserve the life of the said lady Queen of Scotland, which the said lord king will receive as the greatest pleasure your Majesty could do him; while, on the contrary, he could not imagine anything which would cause him more displeasure, and which would wound him more, than if he were used harshly with regard to the said lady queen, being what she is to him: and as, madam, the said king our master, your good brother, when for this object he despatched us to your Majesty, had not conceived that it was possible, in any case, to determine so promptly upon such an execution, we implore you, madam, very humbly, before permitting it to go further, to grant us some time in which we can make known to him the state of the affairs of the said Queen of Scotland, in order that before your Majesty takes a final resolution, you may know what it may please his very Christian Majesty to tell you and point out to you on the greatest affair which, in our memory, has been submitted to men's judgment.

Monsieur de Saint-Cyr, who will give these presents to your Majesty, will bring us, if it pleases you, your good reply.

"London, this 16th day of December 1586.

"(Signed) DE BELLIEVRE,

"And DE L'AUBESPINE CHATEAUNEUF."

The same day, M. de Saint-Cyr and the other French lords returned to Richmond to take this letter; but the queen would not receive them, alleging indisposition, so that they were obliged to leave the letter with Walsingham, her first Secretary of State, who promised them to send the queen's answer the following day.

In spite of this promise, the French lords waited two days more: at last, on the second day, towards evening, two English gentlemen sought out M. de Fellievre in London, and, viva voce, without any letter to confirm what they were charged to say, announced to him, on behalf of their queen, that in reply to the letter that they had written her, and to do justice to the desire they had shown to obtain for the condemned a reprieve during which they would make known the decision to the King of France, her Majesty would grant twelve days. As this was Elizabeth's last word, and it was useless to lose time in pressing her further, M. de Genlis was immediately despatched to his Majesty the King of France, to whom, besides the long despatch of M. de Chateauneuf and de Bellievre which he was charged to remit, he was to say 'viva voce' what he had seen and heard relative to the affairs of Queen Mary during the whole time he had been in England.

Henry III responded immediately with a letter

containing fresh instructions for MM. de Chateauneuf and de Bellievre; but in spite of all the haste M. de Genlis could make, he did not reach London till the fourteenth day—that is to say, forty-eight hours after the expiration of the delay granted; nevertheless, as the sentence had not yet been put into execution, MM. de Bellievre and de Chateauneuf set out at once for Greenwich Castle, some miles from London, where the queen was keeping Christmas, to beg her to grant them an audience, in which they could transmit to her Majesty their king's reply; but they could obtain nothing for four or five days; however, as they were not disheartened, and returned unceasingly to the charge, January 6th, MM. de Bellievre and de Chateauneuf were at last sent for by the queen.

As on the first occasion, they were introduced with all the ceremonial in use at that time, and found Elizabeth in an audience-chamber. The ambassadors approached her, greeted her, and M. de Bellievre began to address to her with respect, but at the same time with firmness, his master's remonstrances. Elizabeth listened to them with an impatient air, fidgeting in her seat; then at last, unable to control herself, she burst out, rising and growing red with anger—

"M. de Bellievre," said she, "are you really charged by the king, my brother, to speak to me in such a way?"

"Yes, madam," replied M. de Bellievre, bowing; "I am expressly commanded to do so."

"And have you this command under his hand?" continued Elizabeth.

"Yes, madam," returned the ambassador with the same calmness; "and the king, my master, your good brother, has expressly charged me, in letters signed by his own hand, to make to your Majesty the remonstrances which I have had the honour to address to you."

"Well," cried Elizabeth, no longer containing herself, "I demand of you a copy of that letter, signed by you; and reflect that you will answer for each word that you take away or add."

"Madam," answered M. de Bellievre, "it is not the custom of the kings of France, or of their agents, to forge letters or documents; you will have the copies you require to-morrow morning, and I pledge their accuracy on my honour."

"Enough, sir, enough!" said the queen, and signing to everyone in the room to go out, she remained nearly an hour with MM. de Chateauneuf and de Bellievre. No one knows what passed in that interview, except that the queen promised to send an ambassador to the King of France, who, she promised, would be in Paris, if not before, at least at the same time as M. de Bellievre, and would be the bearer of her final resolve as to the affairs of the Queen of Scotland; Elizabeth then withdrew, giving the French envoys to understand that any fresh attempt they might make to see her would be useless.

On the 13th of January the ambassadors received their passports, and at the same time notice that a vessel of the queen's was awaiting them at Dover.

The very day of their departure a strange incident

occurred. A gentleman named Stafford, a brother of Elizabeth's ambassador to the King of France, presented himself at M. de Trappes's, one of the officials in the French chancellery, telling him that he was acquainted with a prisoner for debt who had a matter of the utmost importance to communicate to him, and that he might pay the greater attention to it, he told him that this matter was connected with the service of the King of France, and concerned the affairs of Queen Mary of Scotland. M. de Trappes, although mistrusting this overture from the first, did not want, in case his suspicions deceived him, to have to reproach himself for any neglect on such a pressing occasion. He repaired, then, with; Mr. Stafford to the prison, where he who wished to converse with him was detained. When he was with him, the prisoner told him that he was locked up for a debt of only twenty crowns, and that his desire to be at liberty was so great that if M. de Chateauneuf would pay that sum for him he would undertake to deliver the Queen of Scotland from her danger, by stabbing Elizabeth: to this proposal, M. de Trappes, who saw the pitfall laid for the French ambassador, was greatly astonished, and said that he was certain that M. de Chateauneuf would consider as very evil every enterprise having as its aim to threaten in any way the life of Queen Elizabeth or the peace of the realm; then, not desiring to hear more, he returned to M. de Chateauneuf and related to him what had just happened. M. de Chateauneuf, who perceived the real cause of this overture, immediately said to Mr. Stafford that he thought it strange that a gentleman like himself should undertake with another gentleman such treachery, and requested him to leave the Embassy at once, and never to set foot there again. Then Stafford withdrew, and, appearing to think himself a lost man, he implored M. de Trappes to allow him to cross the Channel with him and the French envoys. M. de Trappes referred him to M. de Chateauneuf, who answered Mr. Stafford directly that he had not only forbidden him his house, but also all relations with any person from the Embassy, that he must thus very well see that his request could not be granted; he added that if he were not restrained by the consideration he desired to keep for his brother, the Earl of Stafford, his colleague, he would at once denounce his treason to Elizabeth. The same day Stafford was arrested.

After this conference, M. de Trappes set out to rejoin his travelling companions, who were some hours in advance of him, when, on reaching Dover he was arrested in his turn and brought hack to prison in London. Interrogated the same day, M. de Trappes frankly related what had passed, appealing to M. de Chateauneuf as to the truth of what he said.

The day following there was a second interrogatory, and great was his amazement when, on requesting that the one of the day before should be shown him, he was merely shown, according to custom in English law, counterfeit copies, in which were avowals compromising him as well as M. de Chateauneuf: he objected and protested, refused to answer or to sign anything further, and was taken back to the Tower with redoubled precaution, the object of which was the appearance of an important accusation.

Next day, M. de Chateauneuf was summoned before the queen, and there confronted with Stafford, who impudently maintained that he had treated of a plot with M. de Trappes and a certain prisoner for debt—a plot which aimed at nothing less than endangering the Queen's life. M. de Chateauneuf defended himself with the warmth of indignation, but Elizabeth had too great an interest in being unconvinced even to attend to the evidence. She then said to M. de Chateauneuf that his character of ambassador alone prevented her having him arrested like his accomplice M. de Trappes; and immediately despatching, as she had promised, an ambassador to King Henry III, she charged him not to excuse her for the sentence which had just been pronounced and the death which must soon follow, but to accuse M. de Chateauneuf of having taken part in a plot of which the discovery alone had been able to decide her to consent to the death of the Queen of Scotland, certain as she was by experience, that so long as her enemy lived her existence would be hourly threatened.

On the same day, Elizabeth made haste to spread, not only in London, but also throughout England, the rumour of the fresh danger from which she had just escaped, so that, when, two days after the departure of the French envoys, the Scottish ambassadors, who, as one sees, had not used much speed, arrived, the queen answered them that their request came unseasonably, at a time when she had just had proof that, so long as Mary Stuart existed, her own (Elizabeth's) life was in danger. Robert Melville wished to reply to this; but Elizabeth flew into a passion, saying that it was he, Melville, who had given the King of Scotland the bad advice to intercede for his mother, and that if she had such an adviser she would have him beheaded. To which Melville answered—

"That at the risk of his life he would never spare his master good advice; and that, on the contrary, he who would counsel a son to let his mother perish, would deserve to be beheaded."

Upon this reply, Elizabeth ordered the Scotch envoys to withdrew, telling them that she would let them have her answer.

Three or four days passed, and as they heard nothing further, they asked again for a parting audience to hear the last resolve of her to whom they were sent: the queen then decided to grant it, and all passed, as with M. de Bellievre, in recriminations and complaints. Finally, Elizabeth asked them what guarantee they would give for her life in the event of her consenting to pardon the Queen of Scotland. The envoys responded that they were authorised to make pledges in the name of the King of Scotland, their master, and all the lords of his realm, that Mary Stuart should renounce in favour of her son all her claims upon the English crown, and that she should give as security for this undertaking the King of France, and all the princes and lords, his relations and friends.

To this answer, the queen, without her usual presence of mind, cried, "What are you saying, Melville? That would be to arm my enemy with two claims, while he has only one".

"Does your Majesty then regard the king, my master, as your enemy?" replied Melville. "He believed himself happier, madam, and thought he was your ally."

"No, no," Elizabeth said, blushing; "it is a way of speaking: and if you find a means of reconciling everything, gentlemen, to prove to you, on the contrary, that I regard King James VI as my good and faithful ally, I am quite ready to incline to mercy. Seek, then, on your side" added she, "while I seek on mine."

With these words, she went out of the room, and the ambassadors retired, with the light of the hope of which she had just let them catch a glimpse.

The same evening, a gentleman at the court sought out the Master of Gray, the head of the Embassy, as if to pay him a civil visit, and while conversing said to him, "That it was very difficult to reconcile the safety of Queen Elizabeth with the life of her prisoner; that besides, if the Queen of Scotland were pardoned, and she or her son ever came to the English throne, there would be no security for the lords commissioners who had voted her death; that there was then only one way of arranging everything, that the King of Scotland should himself give up his claims to the kingdom of England; that otherwise, according to him, there was no security for Elizabeth in saving the life of the Scottish queen". The Master of Gray then, looking at him fixedly, asked him if his sovereign had charged him to come to him with this talk. But the gentleman denied it, saying that all this was on his own account and in the way of opinion.

Elizabeth received the envoys from Scotland once more, and then told them—

"That after having well considered, she had found no way of saving the life of the Queen of Scotland while securing her own, that accordingly she could not grant it to them". To this declaration, the Master of Gray replied: "That since it was thus, he was, in this case, ordered by his master to say that they protested in the name of King James that all that had been done against his mother was of no account, seeing that Queen Elizabeth had no authority over a queen, as she was her equal in rank and birth; that accordingly they declared that immediately after their return, and when their master should know the result of their mission, he would assemble his Parliament and send messengers to all the Christian princes, to take counsel with them as to what could be done to avenge her whom they could not save."

Then Elizabeth again flew into a passion, saying that they had certainly not received from their king a mission to speak to her in such a way; but they thereupon offered to give her this protest in writing under their signatures; to which Elizabeth replied that she would send an ambassador to arrange all that with her good friend and ally, the King of Scotland. But the envoys then said that their master would not listen to anyone before their return. Upon which Elizabeth begged them not to go away at once, because she had not yet come to her final decision upon this matter. On the evening following this audience, Lord Hingley having come to see the Master of Gray, and having seemed to notice some handsome pistols which came from Italy, Gray, directly he had gone, asked this nobleman's cousin to take them to him as a gift from him. Delighted with this pleasant commission, the young man wished to perform it the same evening, and went to the queen's palace, where his relative was staying, to give him the present which he had been told to take to him. But hardly had he passed through a few rooms than he was arrested, searched, and the arms he was taking were found upon him. Although these were not loaded, he was immediately arrested; only he was not taken to the Tower, but kept a prisoner in his own room.

Next day there was a rumour that the Scotch ambassadors had wanted to assassinate the queen in their turn, and that pistols, given by the Master of Gray himself, had been found on the assassin.

This bad faith could not but open the envoys' eyes. Convinced at last that they could do nothing for poor Mary Stuart, they left her to her fate, and set out next day for Scotland.

Scarcely were they gone than Elizabeth sent her secretary, Davison, to Sir Amyas Paulet. He was instructed to sound him again with regard to the prisoner; afraid, in spite of herself, of a public execution, the queen had reverted to her former ideas of poisoning or assassination; but Sir Amyas Paulet declared that he would let no one have access to Mary but the executioner, who must in addition be the bearer of a warrant perfectly in order, Davison reported this answer to Elizabeth, who, while listening to him, stamped her foot several times, and when he had finished, unable to control herself, cried, "God's death! there's a dainty fellow, always talking of his fidelity and not knowing how to prove it!"

Elizabeth was then obliged to make up her mind. She asked Davison for the warrant; he gave it to her, and, forgetting that she was the daughter of a queen who had died on the scaffold, she signed it without any trace of emotion; then, having affixed to it the great seal of England, "Go," said she, laughing, "tell Walsingham that all is ended for Queen Mary; but tell him with precautions, for, as he is ill, I am afraid he will die of grief when he hears it."

The jest was the more atrocious in that Walsingham was known to be the Queen of Scotland's bitterest enemy.

Towards evening of that day, Saturday the 14th, Beale, Walsingham's brother-in-law, was summoned to the palace! The queen gave into his hands the death warrant, and with it an order addressed to the Earls of Shrewsbury, Kent, Rutland, and other noblemen in the neighbourhood of Fotheringay, to be present at the execution. Beale took with him the London executioner, whom Elizabeth had had dressed in black velvet for this great occasion; and set out two hours after he had received his warrant.

CHAPTER IX

Queen Mary had known the decree of the commissioners these two months. The very day it had been pronounced she had learned the news through her chaplain, whom they had allowed her to see this once only. Mary Stuart had taken advantage of this visit to give him three letters she had just written-one for Pope Sixtus V, the other to Don Bernard Mendoza, the third to the Duke of Guise. Here is that last letter:—

14th December, 1586

"My Good Cousin, whom I hold dearest in the world, I bid you farewell, being prepared to be put to death by an unjust judgment, and to a death such as no one of our race, thanks to God, and never a queen, and still less one of my rank, has ever suffered. But, good cousin, praise the Lord; for I was useless to the cause of God and of His Church in this world, prisoner as I was; while, on the contrary, I hope that my death will bear witness to my constancy in the faith and to my willingness to suffer for the maintenance and the restoration of the Catholic Church in this unfortunate island. And though never has executioner dipped his hand in our blood, have no shame of it, my friend; for the judgment of heretics who have no authority over me, a free queen, is profitable in the sight of God to the children of His Church. If I adhered, moreover, to what they propose to me, I should not suffer this stroke. All of our house have been persecuted by this sect, witness your good father, through whose intercession I hope to be received with mercy by the just judge. I commend to you, then, my poor servants, the discharge of my debts, and the founding of some annual mass for my soul, not at your expense, but that you may make the arrangements, as you will be required when you learn my wishes through my poor and faithful servants, who are about to witness my last tragedy. God prosper you, your wife, children, brothers and cousins, and above all our chief, my good brother and cousin, and all his. The blessing of God and that which I shall give to my children be on yours, whom I do not commend less to God than my own son, unfortunate and ill-treated as he is. You will receive some rings from me, which will remind you to pray God for the soul of your poor cousin, deprived of all help and counsel except that of the Lord, who gives me strength and courage to alone to resist so many wolves howling after me. To God be the glory.

"Believe particularly what will be told you by a person who will give you a ruby ring from me; for I take it on my conscience that the truth will be told you of what I have charged him to tell, and especially in what concerns my poor servants and the share of any. I commend this person to you for his simple sincerity and honesty, that he may be placed in some good place. I have chosen him as the least partial and as the one who will most simply bring you my commands. Ignore, I beg you, that he told you anything in particular; for envy might injure him. I have suffered a great deal for two years and more, and have not been able to let you know, for an important reason. God be praised for all, and give you grace to persevere in the service of His Church as long as you live, and never may this honour pass from our race, while so many men and women are ready to shed their blood to maintain the fight for the faith, all other worldly considerations set aside. And as to me, I esteem myself born on both father's and mother's sides, that I should offer up my blood for this cause, and I have no intention of degenerating. Jesus, crucified for us, and all the holy martyrs, make us by their intercession worthy of the voluntary offering we make of our bodies to their glory!

"From Fotheringay, this Thursday, 24th November.

"They have, thinking to degrade me, pulled down my canopy of state, and since then my keeper has come to offer to write to their queen, saying this deed was not done by his order, but by the advice of some of the Council. I have shown them instead of my arms on the said canopy the cross of Our Lord. You will hear all this; they have been more gentle since.—Your affectionate cousin and perfect friend,

"MARY, Queen of Scotland, Dowager of France"

From this day forward, when she learned the sentence delivered by the commissioners, Mary Stuart no longer preserved any hope; for as she knew Elizabeth's pardon was required to save her, she looked upon herself thenceforward as lost, and only concerned herself with preparing to die well. Indeed, as it had happened to her sometimes, from the cold and damp in her prisons, to become crippled for some time in all her limbs, she was afraid of being so when they would come to take her, which would prevent her going resolutely to the scaffold, as she was counting on doing. So, on Saturday the 14th February, she sent for her doctor, Bourgoin, and asked him, moved by a presentiment that her death was at hand, she said, what she must do to prevent the return of the pains which crippled her. He replied that it would be good for her to medicine herself with fresh herbs. "Go, then," said the queen, "and ask Sir Amyas Paulet from me permission to seek them in the fields."

Bourgoin went to Sir Amyas, who, as he himself was troubled with sciatica, should have understood better than anyone the need of the remedies for which the queen asked. But this request, simple as it was, raised great difficulties. Sir Amyas replied that he could do nothing without referring to his companion, Drury; but that paper and ink might be brought, and that he, Master Bourgoin, could then make a list of the needful plants, which they would try to procure. Bourgoin answered that he did not know English well enough, and that the village apothecaries did not know enough Latin, for him to risk the queen's life for some error by himself or others. Finally, after a thousand hesitations, Paulet allowed Bourgoin to go out, which he did, accompanied by the apothecary Gorjon; so that the following day the queen was able to begin to doctor herself.

Mary Stuart's presentiments had not deceived her: Tuesday, February 17th, at about two o'clock in the afternoon, the Earls of Kent and Shrewsbury, and Beale sent word to the queen that they desired to speak with her. The queen answered that she was ill and in bed, but that if notwithstanding what they had to tell her was a matter of importance, and they would give her a little time, she would get up. They made answer that the communication they had to make admitted of no delay, that they begged her then to make ready; which the queen immediately did, and rising from her bed and cloaking herself, she went and seated herself at a little table, on the same spot where she was wont to be great part of the day.

Then the two earls, accompanied by Beale, Arnyas Paulet, and Drue Drury, entered. Behind them, drawn by curiosity, full of terrible anxiety, came her dearest ladies and most cherished servants. These were, of womenkind, the Misses Renee de Really, Gilles Mowbray, Jeanne Kennedy, Elspeth Curle, Mary Paget, and Susan Kercady; and of menkind, Dominique Bourgoin her doctor, Pierre Gorjon her apothecary, Jacques Gervais her surgeon, Annibal Stewart her footman, Dither Sifflart her butler, Jean Laudder her baker, and Martin Huet her carver.

Then the Earl of Shrewsbury, with head bared like all those present, who remained thus as long as they were in the queen's room, began to say in English, addressing Mary—

"Madam, the Queen of England, my august mistress, has sent me to you, with the Earl of Kent and Sir Robert Beale, here present, to make known to you that after having honourably proceeded in the inquiry into the deed of which you are accused and found guilty, an inquiry which has already been submitted to your Grace by Lord Buckhurst, and having delayed as long as it was in her power the execution of the sentence, she can no longer withstand the importunity of her subjects, who press her to carry it out, so great and loving is their fear for her. For this purpose we have come the bearers of a commission, and we beg very humbly, madam, that it may please you to hear it read."

"Read, my lord; I am listening," replied Mary Stuart, with the greatest calmness. Then Robert Beale unrolled the said commission, which was on parchment, sealed with the Great Seal in yellow wax, and read as follows:

"Elizabeth, by the grace of God, Queen of England, France, and Ireland, etc., to our beloved and faithful cousins, George, Earl of Shrewsbury, Grand Marshal of England; Henry, Earl of Kent; Henry, Earl of Derby; George, Earl of Cumberland; Henry, Earl of Pembroke, greeting: [The Earls of Cumberland, Derby, and Pembroke did not attend to the queen's orders, and were present neither at the reading of the sentence nor at the execution.]

"Considering the sentence by us given, and others of our Council, nobility, and judges, against the former Queen of Scotland, bearing the name of Mary, daughter and heiress of James v, King of Scotland, commonly called Queen of Scotland and Dowager of France, which sentence all the estates of our realm in our last Parliament assembled not only concluded, but, after mature deliberation, ratified as being just and reasonable; considering also the urgent prayer and request of our subjects, begging us and pressing us to proceed to the publication thereof, and to carry it into execution against her person, according as they judge it duly merited, adding in this place that her detention was and would be daily a certain and evident danger, not only to our life, but also to themselves and their posterity, and to the public weal of this realm, as much on account of the Gospel and the true religion of Christ as of the peace and tranquillity of this State, although the said sentence has been frequently delayed, so that even until this time we abstained from issuing the commission to execute it: yet, for the complete satisfaction of the said demands made by the Estates of our Parliament, through which daily we hear that all our friends and subjects, as well as the nobility, the wisest, greatest, and most pious, nay, even those of inferior condition, with all humility and affection from the care they have of our life, and consequently from the fear they have of the destruction of the present divine and happy state of the realm if we spare the final execution, consenting and desiring the said execution; though the general and continual demands, prayers, counsels, and advice were in such things contrary to our natural inclination; yet, being convinced of the urgent weight of their continual intercessions tending to the safety of our person, and also to the public and private state of our realm, we have at last consented and suffered that justice have its course, and for its execution, considering the singular confidence we have in your fidelity and loyalty together for the love and affection that you have toward us, particularly to the safe-guarding of our person and our country of which you are very noble and chief members; we summon, and, for the discharge of it we enjoin you, that at sight of these presents you go to the castle of Fotheringay, where the former Queen of Scotland is, in the care of our friend and faithful servant and counsellor, Sir Amyas Paulet, and there take into your keeping and do that by your command execution be done on her person, in the presence of yourselves and the said Sir Amyas Paulet, and of all the other officers of justice whom you command to be there: in the meantime we have for this end and this execution given warrant in such a way and manner, and in such a time and place, and by such persons, that you five, four, three, or two, find expedient in your discretion; notwithstanding all laws, statutes, and ordinances whatsoever, contrary to these presents, sealed with our Great Seal of England, which will serve for each of you, and all those who are present, or will make by your order anything pertaining to the execution aforesaid full and sufficient discharge for ever.

"Done and given in our house at Greenwich, the first day of February (10th February New Style), in the twenty-ninth year of our reign."

Mary listened to this reading with great calmness and great dignity; then, when it was ended, making the sign of the cross—

"Welcome," said she, "to all news which comes in the name of God! Thanks, Lord, for that You deign to put an end to all the ills You have seen me suffer for nineteen years and more."

"Madam," said the Earl of Kent, "have no ill-will towards us on account of your death; it was necessary to the peace of the State and the progress of the new religion."

"So," cried Mary with delight, "so I shall have the happiness of dying for the faith of my fathers; thus God deigns to grant me the glory of martyrdom. Thanks, God," added she, joining her hands with less excitement but with more piety, "thanks that You have deigned to destine for me such an end, of which I was not worthy. That, O my God, is indeed a proof of Your love, and an assurance that You will receive me in the number of Your servants; for although this sentence had been notified to me, I was afraid, from the manner in which they have dealt with me for nineteen years, of not yet being so near as I am to such a happy end, thinking that your queen would not dare to lay a hand on me, who, by the grace of God, am a queen as she is, the daughter of a queen as she is, crowned as she is, her near relative, granddaughter of King Henry VII, and who has had the honour of being Queen of France, of which I am still Dowager; and this fear was so much the greater," added she, laying her hand on a New Testament which was near her on the little table, "that, I swear on this holy book, I have never attempted, consented to, or even desired the death of my sister, the Queen of England."

"Madam," replied the Earl of Kent, taking a step towards her and pointing to the New Testament; "this book on which you have sworn is not genuine, since it is the papist version; consequently, your oath cannot be considered as any more genuine than the book on which it has been taken."

"My lord," answered the queen, "what you say may befit you, but not me, who well know that this book is the true and faithful version of the word of the Lord, a version made by a very wise divine, a very good man, and approved by the Church."

"Madam," the Earl of Kent returned, "your Grace stopped at what you were taught in your youth, without inquiry as to whether it was good or bad: it is not surprising, then, that you have remained in your error, for want of having heard anyone who could make known the truth to you; this is why, as your Grace has but a few hours longer to remain in this world, and consequently has no time to lose, with your permission we shall send for the Dean of Peterborough, the most learned man there is on the subject of religion, who, with his word, will prepare you for your salvation, which you risk to our great grief and that of our august queen, by all the papistical follies, abominations, and childish nonsense which keep Catholics away from the holy word of God and the knowledge of the truth."

"You mistake, my lord," replied the queen gently, "if you have believed that I have grown up careless in the faith of my fathers, and without seriously occupying myself with a matter so important as religion. I have, on the contrary, spent my life with learned and wise men who taught me what one must learn on this subject, and I have sustained myself by reading their works, since the means of hearing them has been taken from me. Besides, never having doubted in my lifetime, doubt is not likely to seize me in my death-hour. And there is the Earl of Shrewsbury, here present, who will tell you that, since my arrival in England, I have, for an entire

Lent, of which I repent, heard your wisest doctors, without their arguments having made any impression on my mind. It will be useless, then, my lord," she added, smiling, "to summon to one so hardened as I the Dean of Peterborough, learned as he is. The only thing I ask you in exchange, my lord, and for which I shall be grateful to you beyond expression, is that you will send me my almoner, whom you keep shut up in this house, to console me and prepare me for death, or, in his stead, another priest, be he who he may; if only a poor priest from a poor village, I being no harder to please than God, and not asking that he have knowledge, provided that he has faith."

"It is with regret, madam," replied the Earl of Kent, "that I find myself obliged to refuse your Grace's, request; but it would be contrary to our religion and our conscience, and we should be culpable in doing it; this is why we again offer you the venerable Dean of Peterborough, certain that your Grace will find more consolation and content in him than in any bishop, priest, or vicar of the Catholic faith."

"Thank you, my lord," said the queen again, "but I have nothing to-do with him, and as I have a conscience free of the crime for which I am about to die, with God's help, martyrdom will take the place of confession for me. And now, I will remind you, my lord, of what you told me yourself, that I have but a few hours to live; and these few hours, to profit me, should be passed in prayer and meditation, and not in idle disputes."

With these words, she rose, and, bowing to the earls, Sir

Robert Beale, Amyas, and Drury, she indictated, by a gesture full of dignity, that she wished to be alone and in peace; then, as they prepared to go out—

"Apropos, my lords," said she, "for what o'clock should I make ready to die?"

"For eight o'clock to-morrow, madam," answered the Earl of Shrewsbury, stammering.

"It is well," said Mary; "but have you not some reply to make me, from my sister Elizabeth, relative to a letter which I wrote to her about a month ago?"

"And of what did this letter treat, if it please you, madam?" asked the Earl of Kent.

"Of my burial and my funeral ceremony, my lord: I asked to be interred in France, in the cathedral church of Rheims, near the late queen my mother."

"That may not be, madam," replied the Earl of Kent; "but do not trouble yourself as to all these details: the queen, my august mistress, will provide for them as is suitable. Has your grace anything else to ask us?"

"I would also like to know," said Mary, "if my servants will be allowed to return, each to his own country, with the little that I can give him; which will hardly be enough, in any case, for the long service they have done me, and the long imprisonment they have borne on my account."

"We have no instructions on that head, madam," the Earl of Kent said, "but we think that an order will be given for this as for the other things, in accordance with your wishes. Is this all that your Grace has to say to us?"

"Yes, my lord," replied the queen, bowing a second time, "and now you may withdraw."

"One moment, my lords, in Heaven's name, one moment!" cried the old physician, coming forward and throwing himself on his knees before the two earls.

"What do you want?" asked Lord Shrewsbury.

"To point out to you, my lords," replied the aged Bourgoin, weeping, "that you have granted the queen but a very short time for such an important matter as this of her life. Reflect, my lords, what rank and degree she whom you have condemned has held among the princes of this earth, and consider if it is well and seemly to treat her as an ordinary condemned person of middling estate. And if not for the sake of this noble queen, my lords, do this for the sake of us her poor servants, who, having had the honour of living near her so long, cannot thus part from her so quickly and without preparation. Besides, my lords, think of it, a woman of her state and position ought to have some time in which to set in order her last affairs. And what will become of her, and of us, if before dying, our mistress has not time to regulate her jointure and her accounts and to put in order her papers and her title-deeds? She has services to reward and offices of piety to perform. She should not neglect the one or the other. Besides, we know that she will only concern herself with us, and, through this, my lords, neglect her own salvation. Grant her, then, a few more days, my lords; and as our mistress is too proud to ask of you such a favour, I ask you in all our names, and implore you not to refuse to poor servants a request which your august queen would certainly not refuse them, if they had the good fortune to be able to lay it at her feet."

"Is it then true, madam," Sir Robert Beale asked, "that you have not yet made a will?"

"I have not, sir," the queen answered.

"In that case, my lords," said Sir Robert Beale, turning to the two earls, "perhaps it would be a good thing to put it off for a day or two."

"Impossible, sir," replied the Earl of Shrewsbury: "the time is fixed, and we cannot change anything, even by a minute, now."

"Enough, Bourgoin, enough," said the queen; "rise, I command you."

Bourgoin obeyed, and the Earl of Shrewsbury, turning to Sir Amyas Paulet, who was behind him—

"Sir Amyas," said he, "we entrust this lady to your keeping: you will charge yourself with her, and keep her safe till our return."

With these words he went out, followed by the Earl of Kent, Sir Robert Beale, Amyas Paulet, and Drury, and the queen remained alone with her servants.

Then, turning to her women with as serene a countenance as if the event which had just taken place was of little importance—

"Well, Jeanne," said she, speaking to Kennedy, "have I not always told you, and was I not right, that at the bottom of their hearts they wanted to do this? and did I not see clearly through all their procedure the end they had in view, and know well enough that I was too great an obstacle to their false religion to be allowed to live? Come," continued she, "hasten supper now, that I may put my affairs in order". Then, seeing that instead of obeying her, her servants were weeping and lamenting, "My children," said she, with a sad smile, but without a tear in her eye, "it is no time for weeping, quite the contrary; for if you love me, you ought to rejoice that the Lord, in making me die for His cause, relieves me from the torments I have endured for nineteen years. As for me, I thank Him for allowing me to die for the glory of His faith and His Church. Let each have patience, then, and while the men prepare supper, we women will pray to God."

The men immediately went out, weeping and sobbing, and the queen and her women fell on their knees. When they had recited some prayers, Mary rose, and sending for all the money she had left, she counted it and divided it into portions, which she put into purses with the name of the destined recipient, in her handwriting, with the money.

At that moment, supper being served, she seated herself at table with her women as usual, the other servants standing or coming and going, her doctor waiting on her at table as he was accustomed since her steward had been taken from her. She ate no more nor less than usual, speaking, throughout supper, of the Earl of Kent, and of the way in which he betrayed himself with respect to religion, by his insisting on wanting to give the queen a pastor instead of a priest. "Happily," she added, laughing, "one more skilful than he was needed to change me". Meanwhile Bourgoin was weeping behind the queen, for he was thinking that he was serving her for the last time, and that she who was eating, talking, and laughing thus, next day at the same hour would be but a cold and insensible corpse.

When the meal was over, the queen sent for all her servants; then; before the table was cleared of anything, she poured out a cup of wine, rose and drank to their health, asking them if they would not drink to her salvation. Then she had a glass given to each one: all kneeled down, and all, says the account from which we borrow these details, drank, mingling their tears with the wine, and asking pardon of the queen for any wrongs they had done her. The queen granted it heartily, and asked them to do as much for her, and to forget her impatient ways, which she begged them to put down to her imprisonment. Then, having given them a long discourse, in which she explained to them their duties to God, and exhorted them to persevere in the Catholic faith, she begged them, after her death, to live together in peace and charity, forgetting all the petty quarrels and disputes which they had had among one another in the past.

This speech ended, the queen rose from table, and desired to go into her wardrobe-room, to see the clothes and jewels she wished to dispose of; but Bourgoin observed that it would be better to have all these separate objects brought into her chamber; that there would be a double advantage in this, she would be less tired for one thing, and the English would not see them for another. This last reason decided her, and while the servants were supping, she had brought into her ante-room, first of all, all her robes, and took the inventory from her wardrobe attendant, and began to write in the margin beside each item the name of the person it was to be given to. Directly, and as fast as she did it, that person to whom it was given took it and put it aside. As for the things which were too personal to her to be thus bestowed, she ordered that they should be sold, and that the purchase-money should be used for her servants' travelling expenses, when they returned to their own countries, well knowing how great the cost would be and that no one would have sufficient means. This memorandum finished, she signed it, and gave it as a discharge to her wardrobe attendant.

Then, that done, she went into her room, where had been brought her rings, her jewels, and her most valuable belongings; inspected them all, one after the other, down to the very least; and distributed them as she had done her robes, so that, present or absent, everyone had something. Then she furthermore gave, to her most faithful people, the jewels she intended for the king and queen of France, for the king her son, for the queen-mother, for Messieurs de Guise and de Lorraine, without forgetting in this distribution any prince or princess among her relatives. She desired, besides, that each should keep the things then in his care, giving her linen to the young lady who looked after it, her silk embroideries to her who took charge of them, her silver plate to her butler, and so on with the rest.

Then, as they were asking her for a discharge, "It is

useless," said she; "you owe an account to me only, and tomorrow, therefore, you will no longer owe it to anyone"; but, as they pointed out that the king her son could claim from them, "You are right," said she; and she gave them what they asked.

That done, and having no hope left of being visited by her confessor, she wrote him this letter:

"I have been tormented all this day on account of my religion, and urged to receive the consolations of a heretic: you will learn, through Bourgoin and the others, that everything they could say on this matter has been useless, that I have faithfully made protestation of the faith in which I wish to die. I requested that you should be allowed to receive my confession and to give me the sacrament, which has been cruelly refused, as well as the removal of my body, and the power to make my will freely; so that I cannot write anything except through their hands, and with the good pleasure of their mistress. For want of seeing you, then, I confess to you my sins in general, as I should have done in particular, begging you, in God's name, to watch and pray this night with me, for the remission of my sins, and to send me your absolution and forgiveness for all the wrongs I have done you. I shall try to see you in their presence, as they permitted it to my steward; and if it is allowed, before all, and on my knees, I shall ask your blessing. Send me the best prayers you know for this night and for to-morrow morning; for the time is short, and I have not the leisure to write; but be calm, I shall recommend you like the rest of my servants, and your benefices above all will be secured to you. Farewell, for I have not much more time. Send to me in writing everything you can find, best for my salvation, in prayers and exhortations, I send you my last little ring."

Directly she had written this letter the queen began to make her will, and at a stroke, with her pen running on and almost without lifting it from the paper, she wrote two large sheets, containing several paragraphs, in which no one was forgotten, present as absent, distributing the little she had with scrupulous fairness, and still more according to need than according to service. The executors she chose were: the Duke of Guise, her first cousin; the Archbishop of Glasgow, her ambassador; the Bishop of Ross, her chaplain in chief; and M. du Ruysseau, her chancellor, all four certainly very worthy of the charge, the first from his authority; the two bishops by piety and conscience, and the last by his knowledge of affairs. Her will finished, she wrote this letter to the King of France:

SIR MY BROTHER-IN-LAW,—Having, by God's permission and for my sins, I believe, thrown myself into the arms of this queen, my cousin, where I have had much to endure for more than twenty years, I am by her and by her Parliament finally condemned to death; and having asked for my papers, taken from me, to make my will, I have not been able to obtain anything to serve me, not even permission to write my last wishes freely, nor leave that after my death my body should be transported, as was my dearest desire, into your kingdom, where I had had the honour of being queen, your sister and your ally. To-day, after dinner, without more respect, my sentence has been declared to me, to be executed to-morrow, like a criminal, at eight o'clock in the morning. I have not the leisure to give you a full account of what has occurred; but if it please you to believe my doctor and these others my distressed servants, you will hear the truth, and that, thanks to God, I despise death, which I protest I receive innocent of every crime, even if I were their subject, which I never was. But my faith in the Catholic religion and my claims to the crown of England are the real causes for my condemnation, and yet they will not allow me to say that it is for religion I die, for my religion kills theirs; and that is so true, that they have taken my chaplain from me, who, although a prisoner in the same castle, may not come either to console me, or to give me the holy sacrament of the eucharist; but, on the contrary, they have made me urgent entreaties to receive the consolations of their minister whom they have brought for this purpose. He who will bring you this letter, and the rest of my servants, who are your subjects for the most part, will bear you witness of the way in which I shall have performed my last act. Now it remains to me to implore you, as a most Christian king, as my brother-in-law, as my ancient ally, and one who has so often done me the honour to protest your friendship for me, to give proof of this friendship, in your virtue and your charity, by helping me in that of which I cannot without you discharge my conscience—that is to say, in rewarding my good distressed servants, by giving them their dues; then, in having prayers made to God for a queen who has been called most Christian, and who dies a Catholic and deprived of all her goods. As to my son, I commend him to you as much as he shall deserve, for I cannot answer for him; but as to my servants, I commend them with clasped hands. I have taken the liberty of sending you two rare stones good for the health, hoping that yours may be perfect during a long life; you will receive them as coming from your very affectionate sister-in-law, at the point of death and giving proof of her, good disposition towards you.

"I shall commend my servants to you in a memorandum, and will order you, for the good of my soul, for whose salvation it will be employed, to pay me a portion of what you owe me, if it please you, and I conjure you for the honour of Jesus, to whom I shall pray to-morrow at my death, that you leave me the wherewithal to found a mass and to perform the necessary charities.

"This Wednesday, two hours after midnight—Your affectionate and good sister, "MARY, R...."

Of all these recommendations, the will and the letters, the queen at once had copies made which she signed, so that, if some should be seized by the English, the others might reach their destination. Bourgoin pointed out to her that she was wrong to be in such a hurry to close them, and that perhaps in two or three hours she would remember that she had left something out. But the queen paid no attention, saying she was sure she had not forgotten anything, and that if she had, she had only time now to pray and to look to her conscience. So she shut up all the several articles in the drawers of a piece of furniture and gave the key to Bourgoin; then sending for a foot-bath, in which she stayed for about ten minutes, she lay down in bed, where she was not seen to sleep, but constantly to repeat prayers or to remain in meditation.

Towards four o'clock in the morning, the queen, who was accustomed, after evening prayers, to have the story of some male or female saint read aloud to her, did not wish to depart from this habit, and, after having hesitated among several for this solemn occasion, she chose the greatest sinner of all, the penitent thief, saying humbly—

"If, great sinner as he was, he has yet sinned less than I, I desire to beg of him, in remembrance of the passion of Jesus Christ; to, have pity on me in the hour of my death, as Our Lord had pity on him."

Then, when the reading was over, she had all her handkerchiefs brought, and chose the finest, which was of delicate cambric all embroidered in gold, to bandage her eyes with.

At daybreak, reflecting that she had only two hours to live, she rose and began dressing, but before she had finished, Bourgoin came into her room, and, afraid lest the absent servants might murmur against the queen, if by chance they were discontented at the will, and might accuse those who had been present of having taken away from their share to add to their own, he begged Mary to send for them all and to read it in their presence; to which Mary agreed, and consented to do so at once.

All the servants were then summoned, and the queen read her testament, saying that it was done of her own free, full and entire will, written and signed with her own hand, and that accordingly she begged those present to give all the help in their power in seeing it carried out without change or omission; then, having read it over, and having received a promise from all, she gave it to Bourgoin, charging him to send it to M. de Guise, her chief executor, and at the same time to forward her letters to the king and her principal papers and memorandums: after this, she had the casket brought in which she had put the purses which we mentioned before; she opened them one after another, and seeing by the ticket within for whom each was intended, she distributed them with her own hand, none of the recipients being aware of their contents. These gifts varied from twenty to three hundred crowns; and to these sums she added seven hundred livres for the poor, namely, two hundred for the poor of England and five hundred for the poor of France; then she gave to each man in her suite two rose nobles to be distributed in alms for her sake, and finally one hundred and fifty crowns to Bourgoin to be divided among them all when they should separate; and thus twenty-six or twenty-seven people had money legacies.

The queen performed all this with great composure and calmness, with no apparent change of countenance; so that it seemed as if she were only preparing for a journey or change of dwelling; then she again bade her servants farewell, consoling them and exhorting them to live in peace, all this while finishing dressing as well and as elegantly as she could.

Her toilet ended, the queen went from her reception-room to her ante-room, where there was an altar set up and arranged, at which, before he had been taken from her, her chaplain used to say mass; and kneeling on the steps, surrounded by all her servants, she began the communion prayers, and when they were ended, drawing from a golden box a host consecrated by Pius V, which she had always scrupulously preserved for the occasion of her death, she told Bourgoin to take it, and, as he was the senior, to take the priest's place, old age being holy and sacred; and in this manner in spite of all the precautions taken to deprive her of it, the queen received the holy sacrament of the eucharist.

This pious ceremony ended, Bourgoin told the queen that in her will she had forgotten three people—Mesdemoiselles Beauregard, de Montbrun, and her chaplain. The queen was greatly astonished at this oversight, which was quite involuntary, and, taking back her will, she wrote her wishes with respect to them in the first empty margin; then she kneeled down again in prayer; but after a moment, as she suffered too much in this position, she rose, and Bourgoin having had brought her a little bread and wine, she ate and drank, and when she had finished, gave him her hand and thanked him for having been present to help her at her last meal as he was accustomed; and feeling stronger, she kneeled down and began to pray again.

Scarcely had she done so, than there was a knocking at the door: the queen understood what was required of her; but as she had not finished praying, she begged those who were come to fetch her to wait a moment, and in a few minutes' she would be ready.

The Earls of Kent and Shrewsbury, remembering the resistance she had made when she had had to go down to the commissioners and appear before the lawyers, mounted some guards in the ante-room where they were waiting themselves, so that they could take her away by force if necessary, should she refuse to come willingly, or should her servants want to defend her; but it is untrue that the two barons entered her room, as some have said. They only set foot there once, on the occasion which we have related, when they came to apprise her of her sentence.

They waited some minutes, nevertheless, as the queen had begged them; then, about eight o'clock, they knocked again, accompanied by the guards; but to their great surprise the door was opened immediately, and they found Mary on her knees in prayer. Upon this, Sir Thomas Andrew, who was at the time sheriff of the county of Nottingham, entered alone, a white wand in his hand, and as everyone stayed on their knees praying, he crossed the room with a slow step and stood behind the queen: he waited a moment there, and as Mary Stuart did not seem to see him—

"Madam," said he, "the earls have sent me to you."

At these words the queen turned round, and at once rising in the middle of her prayer, "Let us go," she replied, and she made ready to follow him; then Bourgoin, taking the cross of black wood with an ivory Christ which was over the altar, said—

"Madam, would you not like to take this little cross?"

"Thank you for having reminded me," Mary answered; "I had intended to, but I forgot". Then, giving it to Annibal Stewart, her footman, that he might present it when she should ask for it, she began to move to the door, and on account of the great pain in her limbs, leaning on Bourgoin, who, as they drew near, suddenly let her go, saying—

"Madam, your Majesty knows if we love you, and all, such as we are, are ready to obey you, should you command us to die for you; but I, I have not the strength to lead you farther; besides, it is not becoming that we, who should be defending you to the last drop of our blood, should seem to be betraying you in giving you thus into the hands of these infamous English."

"You are right, Bourgoin," said the queen; "moreover, my death would be a sad sight for you, which I ought to spare your age and your friendship. Mr. Sheriff," added she, "call someone to support me, for you see that I cannot walk."

The sheriff bowed, and signed to two guards whom he had kept hidden behind the door to lend him assistance in case the queen should resist, to approach and support her; which they at once did; and Mary Stuart went on her way, preceded and followed by her servants weeping and wringing their hands. But at the second door other guards stopped them, telling them they must go no farther. They all cried out against such a prohibition: they said that for the nineteen years they had been shut up with the queen they had always accompanied her wherever she went; that it was frightful to deprive their mistress of their services at the last moment, and that such an order had doubtless been given because they wanted to practise some shocking cruelty on her, of which they desired no witnesses. Bourgoin, who was at their head, seeing that he could obtain nothing by threats or entreaties, asked to speak with the earls; but this claim was not allowed either, and as the servants wanted to pass by force, the soldiers repulsed them with blows of their arquebuses; then, raising her voice—

"It is wrong of you to prevent my servants following me," said the queen, "and I begin to think, like them, that you have some ill designs upon me beyond my death."

The sheriff replied, "Madam, four of your servants are chosen to follow you, and no more; when you have come down, they will be fetched, and will rejoin you."

"What!" said the queen, "the four chosen persons cannot even follow me now?"

"The order is thus given by the earls," answered the sheriff, "and, to my great regret, madam, I can do nothing."

Then the queen turned to them, and taking the cross from Annibal Stewart, and in her other hand her book of Hours and her handkerchief, "My children," said she, "this is one more grief to add to our other griefs; let us bear it like Christians, and offer this fresh sacrifice to God."

At these words sobs and cries burst forth on all sides: the unhappy servants fell on their knees, and while some rolled on the ground, tearing their hair, others kissed her hands, her knees, and the hem of her gown, begging her forgiveness for every possible fault, calling her their mother and bidding her farewell. Finding, no doubt, that this scene was lasting too long, the sheriff made a sign, and the soldiers pushed the men and women back into the room and shut the door on them; still, fast as was the door, the queen none the less heard their cries and lamentations, which seemed, in spite of the guards, as if they would accompany her to the scaffold.

At the stair-head, the queen found Andrew Melville awaiting her: he was the Master of her Household, who had been secluded from her for some time, and who was at last permitted to see her once more to say farewell. The queen, hastening her steps, approached him, and kneeling down to receive his blessing, which he gave her, weeping—

"Melville," said she, without rising, and addressing him as "thou" for the first time, "as thou hast been an honest servant to me, be the same to my son: seek him out directly after my death, and tell him of it in every detail; tell him that I wish him well, and that I beseech God to send him His Holy Spirit."

"Madam," replied Melville, "this is certainly the saddest message with which a man can be charged: no matter, I shall faithfully fulfil it, I swear to you."

"What sayest thou, Melville?" responded the queen, rising; "and what better news canst thou bear, on the contrary, than that I am delivered from all my ills? Tell him that he should rejoice, since the sufferings of Mary Stuart are at an end; tell him that I die a Catholic, constant in my religion, faithful to Scotland and France, and that I forgive those who put me to death. Tell him that I have always desired the union of England and Scotland; tell him, finally, that I have done nothing injurious to his kingdom, to his honour, or to his rights. And thus, good Melville, till we meet again in heaven."

Then, leaning on the old man, whose face was bathed in tears, she descended the staircase, at the foot of which she found the two earls, Sir Henry Talbot, Lord Shrewsbury's son, Amyas Paulet, Drue Drury, Robert Beale, and many gentlemen of the neighbourhood: the queen, advancing towards them without pride, but without humility, complained that her servants had been refused permission to follow her, and asked that it should be granted. The lords conferred together; and a moment after the Earl of Kent inquired which ones she desired to have, saying she might be allowed six. So the queen chose from among the men Bourgoin, Gordon, Gervais, and Didier; and from the women Jeanne Kennedy and Elspeth Curle, the ones she preferred to all, though the latter was sister to the secretary who had betrayed her. But here arose a fresh difficulty, the earls saying that this permission did not extend to women, women not being used to be present at such sights, and when they were, usually upsetting everyone with cries and lamentations, and, as soon as the decapitation was over, rushing to the scaffold to staunch the blood with their handkerchiefs—a most unseemly proceeding.

"My lords," then said the queen, "I answer and promise for my servants, that they will not do any of the things your honours fear. Alas! poor people! they would be very glad to bid me farewell; and I hope that your mistress, being a maiden queen, and accordingly sensitive for the honour of women, has not given you such strict orders that you are unable to grant me the little I ask; so much the more," added she in a profoundly mournful tone, "that my rank should be taken into consideration; for indeed I am your queen's cousin, granddaughter of Henry VII, Queen Dowager of France and crowned Queen of Scotland."

The lords consulted together for another moment, and granted her demands. Accordingly, two guards went up immediately to fetch the chosen individuals.

The queen then moved on to the great hall, leaning on two of Sir Amyas Paulet's gentlemen, accompanied and followed by the earls and lords, the sheriff walking before her, and Andrew Melville bearing her train. Her dress, as carefully chosen as possible, as we have said, consisted of a coif of fine cambric, trimmed with lace, with a lace veil thrown back and falling to the ground behind. She wore a cloak of black stamped satin lined with black taffetas and trimmed in front with sable, with a long train and sleeves hanging to the ground; the buttons were of jet in the shape of acorns and surrounded with pearls, her collar in the Italian style; her doublet was of figured black satin, and underneath she wore stays, laced behind, in crimson satin, edged with velvet of the same colour; a gold cross hung by a pomander chain at her neck, and two rosaries at her girdle: it was thus she entered the great hall where the scaffold was erected.

It was a platform twelve feet wide, raised about two feet

from the floor, surrounded with barriers and covered with black serge, and on it were a little chair, a cushion to kneel on, and a block also covered in black. Just as, having mounted the steps, she set foot on the fatal boards, the executioner came forward, and; asking forgiveness for the duty he was about to perform, kneeled, hiding behind him his axe. Mary saw it, however, and cried—

"Ah! I would rather have been beheaded in the French way, with a sword!..."

"It is not my fault, madam," said the executioner, "if this last wish of your Majesty cannot be fulfilled; but, not having been instructed to bring a sword, and having found this axe here only, I am obliged to use it. Will that prevent your pardoning me, then?"

"I pardon you, my friend," said Mary, "and in proof of it, here is my hand to kiss."

The executioner put his lips to the queen's hand, rose and approached the chair. Mary sat down, and the Earls of Kent and Shrewsbury standing on her left, the sheriff and his officers before her, Amyas Paulet behind, and outside the barrier the lords, knights, and gentlemen, numbering nearly two hundred and fifty, Robert Beale for the second time read the warrant for execution, and as he was beginning the servants who had been fetched came into the hall and placed themselves behind the scaffold, the men mounted upon a bench put back against the wall, and the women kneeling in front of it; and a little spaniel, of which the queen was very fond, came quietly, as if he feared to be driven away, and lay down near his mistress.

The queen listened to the reading of the warrant without seeming to pay much attention, as if it had concerned someone else, and with a countenance as calm and even as joyous as if it had been a pardon and not a sentence of death; then, when Beale had ended, and having ended, cried in a loud voice, "God save Queen Elizabeth!" to which no one made any response, Mary signed herself with the cross, and, rising without any change of expression, and, on the contrary, lovelier than ever—

"My lords," said she, "I am a queen-born sovereign princess, and not subject to law,—a near relation of the Queen of England, and her rightful heir; for a long time I have been a prisoner in this country, I have suffered here much tribulation and many evils that no one had the right to inflict, and now, to crown all, I am about to lose my life. Well, my lords, bear witness that I die in the Catholic faith, thanking God for letting me die for His holy cause, and protesting, to-day as every day, in public as in private, that I have never plotted, consented to, nor desired the queen's death, nor any other thing against her person; but that, on the contrary, I have always loved her, and have always offered her good and reasonable conditions to put an end to the troubles of the kingdom and deliver me from my captivity, without my having ever been honoured with a reply from her; and all this, my lords, you well know. Finally, my enemies have attained their end, which was to put me to death: I do not pardon them less for it than I pardon all those who have attempted anything against me. After my, death, the authors of it will be known. But I die without accusing anyone, for fear the Lord should hear me and avenge me."

Upon this, whether he was afraid that such a speech by so great a queen should soften the assembly too much, or whether he found that all these words were making too much delay, the Dean of Peterborough placed himself before Mary, and, leaning on the barrier—

"Madam," he said, "my much honoured mistress has commanded me to come to you—" But at these words, Mary, turning and interrupting him:

"Mr. Dean," she answered in a loud voice, "I have nothing to do with you; I do not wish to hear you, and beg you to withdraw."

"Madam," said the dean, persisting in spite of this resolve expressed in such firm and precise terms, "you have but a moment longer: change your opinions, abjure your errors, and put your faith in Jesus Christ alone, that you may be saved through Him."

"Everything you can say is useless," replied the queen, "and you will gain nothing by it; be silent, then, I beg you, and let me die in peace."

And as she saw that he wanted to go on, she sat down on the other side of the chair and turned her back to him; but the dean immediately walked round the scaffold till he faced her again; then, as he was going to speak, the queen turned about once more, and sat as at first. Seeing which the Earl of Shrewsbury said—

"Madam, truly I despair that you are so attached to this folly of papacy: allow us, if it please you, to pray for you."

"My lord," the queen answered, "if you desire to pray for me, I thank you, for the intention is good; but I cannot join in your prayers, for we are not of the same religion."

The earls then called the dean, and while the queen, seated in her little chair, was praying in a low tone, he, kneeling on the scaffold steps, prayed aloud; and the whole assembly except the queen and her servants prayed after him; then, in the midst of her orison, which she said with her Agnus Dei round her neck, a crucifix in one hand, and her book of Hours in the other, she fell from her seat on to, her knees, praying aloud in Latin, whilst the others prayed in English, and when the others were silent, she continued in English in her turn, so that they could hear her, praying for the afflicted Church of Christ, for an end to the persecution of Catholics, and for the happiness of her son's reign; then she said, in accents full of faith and fervour, that she hoped to be saved by the merits of Jesus Christ, at the foot of whose cross she was going to shed her blood.

At these words the Earl of Kent could no longer contain himself, and without respect for the sanctity of the moment—

"Oh, madam," said he, "put Jesus Christ in your heart, and reject all this rubbish of popish deceptions."

But she, without listening, went on, praying the saints to intercede with God for her, and kissing the crucifix, she cried—

"Lord! Lord! receive me in Thy arms out stretched on the

cross, and forgive me all my sins!"

Thereupon,—she being again seated in the chair, the Earl of Kent asked her if she had any confession to make; to which she replied that, not being guilty of anything, to confess would be to give herself, the lie.

"It is well," the earl answered; "then, madam, prepare."

The queen rose, and as the executioner approached to assist her disrobe—

"Allow me, my friend," said she; "I know how to do it better than you, and am not accustomed to undress before so many spectators, nor to be served by such valets."

And then, calling her two women, she began to unpin her coiffure, and as Jeanne Kennedy and Elspeth Curle, while performing this last service for their mistress, could not help weeping bitterly—

"Do not weep," she said to them in French; "for I have promised and answered for you."

With these words, she made the sign of the cross upon the forehead of each, kissed them, and recommended them to pray for her.

Then the queen began to undress, herself assisting, as she was wont to do when preparing for bed, and taking the gold cross from her neck, she wished to give it to Jeanne, saying to the executioner—

"My friend, I know that all I have upon me belongs to you; but this is not in your way: let me bestow it, if you please, on this young lady, and she will give you twice its value in money."

But the executioner, hardly allowing her to finish, snatched it from her hands with—

"It is my right."

The queen was not moved much by this brutality, and went on taking off her garments until she was simply in her petticoat.

Thus rid of all her garb, she again sat down, and Jeanne Kennedy approaching her, took from her pocket the handkerchief of gold-embroidered cambric which she had prepared the night before, and bound her eyes with it; which the earls, lords; and gentlemen looked upon with great surprise, it not being customary in England, and as she thought that she was to be beheaded in the French way— that is to say, seated in the chair—she held herself upright, motionless, and with her neck stiffened to make it easier for the executioner, who, for his part, not knowing how to proceed, was standing, without striking, axe in hand: at last the man laid his hand on the queen's head, and drawing her forward, made her fall on her knees: Mary then understood what was required of her, and feeling for the block with her hands, which were still holding her book of Hours and her crucifix, she laid her neck on it, her hands joined beneath her chin, that she might pray till the last moment: the executioner's assistant drew them away, for fear they should be cut off with her head; and as the queen was saying, "In manes teas, Domine," the executioner raised his axe, which was simply an axe far chopping wood, and struck the first blow, which hit too high, and piercing the skull, made the crucifix and the book fly from the condemned's hands by its violence, but which did not sever the head. However, stunned with the blow, the queen made no movement, which gave the executioner time to redouble it; but still the head did not fall, and a third stroke was necessary to detach a shred of flesh which held it to the shoulders.

At last, when the head was quite severed, the executioner held it up to show to the assembly, saying:

"God save Queen Elizabeth!"

"So perish all Her Majesty's enemies!" responded the Dean of Peterborough.

"Amen," said the Earl of Kent; but he was the only one: no other voice could respond, for all were choked with sobs.

At that moment the queen's headdress falling, disclosed her hair, cut very short, and as white as if she had been aged seventy: as to her face, it had so changed during her death-agony that no one would have recognised it had he not known it was hers. The spectators cried out aloud at this sign; for, frightful to see, the eyes were open, and the lids went on moving as if they would still pray, and this muscular movement lasted for more than a quarter of an hour after the head had been cut off.

The queen's servants had rushed upon the scaffold, picking up the book of Hours and the crucifix as relics; and Jeanne Kennedy, remembering the little dog who had come to his mistress, looked about for him on all sides, seeking him and calling him, but she sought and called in vain. He had disappeared.

At that moment, as one of the executioners was untying the queen's garters, which were of blue satin embroidered in silver, he saw the poor little animal, which had hidden in her petticoat, and which he was obliged to bring out by force; then, having escaped from his hands, it took refuge between the queen's shoulders and her head, which the executioner had laid down near the trunk. Jeanne took him then, in spite of his howls, and carried him away, covered with blood; for everyone had just been ordered to leave the hall. Bourgoin and Gervais stayed behind, entreating Sir Amyas Paulet to let them take the queen's heart, that they might carry it to France, as they had promised her; but they were harshly refused and pushed out of the hall, of which all the doors were closed, and there there remained only the executioner and the corpse.

Brantome relates that something infamous took place there!

CHAPTER X

Two hours after the execution, the body and the head were taken into the same hall in which Mary Stuart had appeared before the commissioners, set down on a table round which the judges had sat, and covered over with a black serge cloth; and there remained till three o'clock in the afternoon, when Waters the doctor from Stamford and the surgeon from Fotheringay village came to open and embalm them—an operation which they carried out under the eyes of Amyas Paulet and his soldiers, without any respect for the rank and sex of the poor corpse, which was thus exposed to the view of anyone who wanted to see it: it is true that this indignity did not fulfil its proposed aim; for a rumour spread about that the queen had swollen limbs and was dropsical, while, on the contrary, there was not one of the spectators but was obliged to confess that he had never seen the body of a young girl in the bloom of health purer and lovelier than that of Mary Stuart, dead of a violent death after nineteen years of suffering and captivity.

When the body was opened, the spleen was in its normal state, with the veins a little livid only, the lungs yellowish in places, and the brain one-sixth larger than is usual in persons of the same age and sex; thus everything promised a long life to her whose end had just been so cruelly hastened.

A report having been made of the above, the body was embalmed after a fashion, put in a leaden coffin and that in another of wood, which was left on the table till the first day of August—that is, for nearly five months—before anyone was allowed to come near it; and not only that, but the English having noticed that Mary Stuart's unhappy servants, who were still detained as prisoners, went to look at it through the keyhole, stopped that up in such a way that they could not even gaze at the coffin enclosing the body of her whom they had so greatly loved.

However, one hour after Mary Stuart's death, Henry Talbot, who had been present at it, set out at full speed for London, carrying to Elizabeth the account of her rival's death; but at the very first lines she read, Elizabeth, true to her character, cried out in grief and indignation, saying that her orders had been misunderstood, that there had been too great haste, and that all this was the fault of Davison the Secretary of State, to whom she had given the warrant to keep till she had made up her mind, but not to send to Fotheringay. Accordingly, Davison was sent to the Tower and condemned to pay a fine of ten thousand pounds sterling, for having deceived the queen. Meanwhile, amid all this grief, an embargo was laid on all vessels in all the ports of the realm, so that the news of the death should not reach abroad, especially France, except through skilful emissaries who could place the execution in the least unfavourable light for Elizabeth. At the same time the scandalous popular festivities which had marked the announcement of the sentence again celebrated the tidings of the execution. London was illuminated, bonfires lit, and the enthusiasm was such that the French Embassy was broken into and wood taken to revive the fires when they began to die down.

Crestfallen at this event, M. de Chateauneuf was still shut up at the Embassy, when, a fortnight later, he received an invitation from Elizabeth to visit her at the country house of the Archbishop of Canterbury. M. de Chateauneuf went thither with the firm resolve to say no word to her on what had happened; but as soon as she saw him, Elizabeth, dressed in black, rose, went to him, and, overwhelming him with kind attentions, told him that she was ready to place all the strength of her kingdom at Henry III's disposal to help him put down the League. Chateauneuf received all these offers with a cold and severe expression, without saying, as he had promised himself, a single word about the event which had put both the queen and himself into mourning. But, taking him by the hand, she drew him aside, and there, with deep sighs, said—

"Ah! sir, since I saw you the greatest misfortune which could befall me has happened: I mean the death of my good sister, the Queen of Scotland, of which I swear by God Himself, my soul and my salvation, that I am perfectly innocent. I had signed the order, it is true; but my counsellors have played me a trick for which I cannot calm myself; and I swear to God that if it were not for their long service I would have them beheaded. I have a woman's frame, sir, but in this woman's frame beats a man's heart."

Chateauneuf bowed without a response; but his letter to Henry III and Henry's answer prove that neither the one nor the other was the dupe of this female Tiberius.

Meanwhile, as we have said, the unfortunate servants were prisoners, and the poor body was in that great hall waiting for a royal interment. Things remained thus, Elizabeth said, to give her time to order a splendid funeral for her good sister Mary, but in reality because the queen dared not place in juxtaposition the secret and infamous death and the public and royal burial; then, was not time needed for the first reports which it pleased Elizabeth to spread to be credited before the truth should be known by the mouths of the servants? For the queen hoped that once this careless world had made up its mind about the death of the Queen of Scots, it would not take any further trouble to change it. Finally, it was only when the warders were as tired as the prisoners, that Elizabeth, having received a report stating that the ill-embalmed body could no longer be kept, at last ordered the funeral to take place.

Accordingly, after the 1st of August, tailors and dressmakers arrived at Fotheringay Castle, sent by Elizabeth, with cloth and black silk stuffs, to clothe in mourning all Mary's servants. But they refused, not having waited for the Queen of England's bounty, but having made their funeral garments at their own expense, immediately after their mistress's death. The tailors and dressmakers, however, none the less set so actively to work that on the 7th everything was finished.

Next day, at eight o'clock in the evening, a large chariot, drawn by four horses in mourning trappings, and covered with black velvet like the chariot, which was, besides, adorned with little streamers on which were embroidered the arms of Scotland, those of the queen, and the arms of Aragon, those of Darnley, stopped at the gate of Fotheringay Castle. It was followed by the herald king, accompanied by twenty gentlemen on horseback, with their servants and lackeys, all dressed in mourning, who, having alighted, mounted with his whole train into the room where the body lay, and had it brought down and put into the chariot with all possible respect, each of the spectators standing with bared head and in profound silence.

This visit caused a great stir among the prisoners, who debated a while whether they ought not to implore the favour of being allowed to follow their mistress's body, which they could not and should not let go alone thus; but just as they were about to ask permission to speak to the herald king, he entered the room where they were assembled, and told them that he was charged by his mistress, the august Queen of England, to give the Queen of Scotland the most honourable funeral he could; that, not wishing to fail in such a high undertaking, he had already made most of the preparations for the ceremony, which was to take place on the 10th of August, that is to say, two days later,—but that the leaden shell in which the body was enclosed being very heavy, it was better to move it beforehand, and that night, to where the grave was dug, than to await the day of the interment itself; that thus they might be easy, this burial of the shell being only a preparatory ceremony; but that if some of them would like to accompany the corpse, to see what was done with it, they were at liberty, and that those who stayed behind could follow the funeral pageant, Elizabeth's positive desire being that all, from first to last, should be present in the funeral procession. This assurance calmed the unfortunate prisoners, who deputed Bourgoin, Gervais, and six others to follow their mistress's body: these were Andrew Melville, Stewart, Gorjon, Howard, Lauder, and Nicholas Delamarre.

At ten o'clock at night they set out, walking behind the chariot, preceded by the herald, accompanied by men on foot, who carried torches to light the way, and followed by twenty gentlemen and their servants. In this manner, at two o'clock in the morning, they reached Peterborough, where there is a splendid cathedral built by an ancient Saxon king, and in which, on the left of the choir, was already interred good Queen Catharine of Aragon, wife of Henry VIII, and where was her tomb, still decked with a canopy bearing her arms.

On arriving, they found the cathedral all hung with black, with a dome erected in the middle of the choir, much in the way in which 'chapelles ardentes' are set up in France, except that there were no lighted candles round it. This dome was covered with black velvet, and overlaid with the arms of Scotland and Aragon, with streamers like those on the chariot yet again repeated. The state coffin was already set up under this dome: it was a bier, covered like the rest in black velvet fringed with silver, on which was a pillow of the same supporting a royal crown.

To the right of this dome, and in front of the burial-place of Queen Catharine of Aragon, Mary of Scotland's sepulchre had been dug: it was a grave of brick, arranged to be covered later with a slab or a marble tomb, and in which was to be deposited the coffin, which the Bishop of Peterborough, in his episcopal robes, but without his mitre, cross, or cope, was awaiting at the door, accompanied by his dean and several other clergy. The body was brought into the cathedral, without chant or prayer, and was let down into the tomb amid a profound silence. Directly it was placed there, the masons, who had stayed their hands, set to work again, closing the grave level with the floor, and only leaving an opening of about a foot and a half, through which could be seen what was within, and through which could be thrown on the coffin, as is customary at the obsequies of kings, the broken staves of the officers and the ensigns and banners with their arms. This nocturnal ceremony ended, Melville, Bourgoin, and the other deputies were taken to the bishop's palace, where the persons appointed to take part in the funeral procession were to assemble, in number more than three hundred and fifty, all chosen, with the exception of the servants, from among the authorities, the nobility, and Protestant clergy.

The day following, Thursday, August the 9th, they began to hang the banqueting halls with rich and sumptuous stuffs, and that in the sight of Melville, Bourgoin, and the others, whom they had brought thither, less to be present at the interment of Queen Mary than to bear witness to the magnificence of Queen Elizabeth. But, as one may suppose, the unhappy prisoners were indifferent to this splendour, great and extraordinary as it was.

On Friday, August 10th, all the chosen persons assembled at the bishop's palace: they ranged themselves in the appointed order, and turned their steps to the cathedral, which was close by. When they arrived there, they took the places assigned them in the choir, and the choristers immediately began to chant a funeral service in English and according to Protestant rites. At the first words of this service, when he saw it was not conducted by Catholic priests, Bourgoin left the cathedral, declaring that he would not be present at such sacrilege, and he was followed by all Mary's servants, men and women, except Melville and Barbe Mowbray, who thought that whatever the tongue in which one prayed, that tongue was heard by the Lord. This exit created great scandal; but the bishop preached none the less.

The sermon ended, the herald king went to seek Bourgoin and his companions, who were walking in the cloisters, and told them that the almsgiving was about to begin, inviting them to take part in this ceremony; but they replied that being Catholics they could not make offerings at an altar of which they disapproved. So the herald king returned, much put out at the harmony of the assembly being disturbed by this dissent; but the alms-offering took place no less than the sermon. Then, as a last attempt, he sent to them again, to tell them that the service was quite over, and that accordingly they might return for the royal ceremonies, which belonged only to the religion of the dead; and this time they consented;

but when they arrived, the staves were broken, and the banners thrown into the grave through the opening that the workmen had already closed.

Then, in the same order in which it had come, the procession returned to the palace, where a splendid funeral repast had been prepared. By a strange contradiction, Elizabeth, who, having punished the living woman as a criminal, had just treated the dead woman as a queen, had also wished that the honours of the funeral banquet should be for the servants, so long forgotten by her. But, as one can imagine, these ill accommodated themselves to that intention, did not seem astonished at this luxury nor rejoiced at this good cheer, but, on the contrary, drowned their bread and wine in tears, without otherwise responding to the questions put to them or the honours granted them. And as soon as the repast was ended, the poor servants left Peterborough and took the road back to Fotheringay, where they heard that they were free at last to withdraw whither they would. They did not need to be told twice; for they lived in perpetual fear, not considering their lives safe so long as they remained in England. They therefore immediately collected all their belongings, each taking his own, and thus went out of Fotheringay Castle on foot, Monday, 13th August, 1587.

Bourgoin went last: having reached the farther side of the drawbridge, he turned, and, Christian as he was, unable to forgive Elizabeth, not for his own sufferings, but for his mistress's, he faced about to those regicide walls, and, with hands outstretched to them, said in a loud and threatening voice, those words of David: "Let vengeance for the blood of Thy servants, which has been shed, O Lord God, be acceptable in Thy sight". The old man's curse was heard, and inflexible history is burdened with Elizabeth's punishment.

We said that the executioner's axe, in striking Mary Stuart's head, had caused the crucifix and the book of Hours which she was holding to fly from her hands. We also said that the two relics had been picked up by people in her following. We are not aware of what became of the crucifix, but the book of Hours is in the royal library, where those curious about these kinds of historical souvenirs can see it: two certificates inscribed on one of the blank leaves of the volume demonstrate its authenticity. These are they:

FIRST CERTIFICATE

"We the undersigned Vicar Superior of the strict observance of the Order of Cluny, certify that this book has been entrusted to us by order of the defunct Dom Michel Nardin, a professed religious priest of our said observance, deceased in our college of Saint-Martial of Avignon, March 28th, 1723, aged about eighty years, of which he has spent about thirty among us, having lived very religiously: he was a German by birth, and had served as an officer in the army a long time.

"He entered Cluny, and made his profession there, much detached from all this world's goods and honours; he only kept, with his superior's permission, this book, which he knew had been in use with Mary Stuart, Queen of England and Scotland, to the end of her life.

"Before dying and being parted from his brethren, he requested that, to be safely remitted to us, it should be sent us by mail, sealed. Just as we have received it, we have begged M. L'abbe Bignon, councillor of state and king's librarian, to accept this precious relic of the piety of a Queen of England, and of a German officer of her religion as well as of ours.

"(Signed)BROTHER GERARD PONCET, "Vicar-General Superior."

SECOND CERTIFICATE

"We, Jean-Paul Bignon, king's librarian, are very happy to have an opportunity of exhibiting our zeal, in placing the said manuscript in His Majesty's library.

"8th July, 1724."

"(Signed) JEAN-PAUL BIGNAN."

This manuscript, on which was fixed the last gaze of the Queen of Scotland, is a duodecimo, written in the Gothic character and containing Latin prayers; it is adorned with miniatures set off with gold, representing devotional subjects, stories from sacred history, or from the lives of saints and martyrs. Every page is encircled with arabesques mingled with garlands of fruit and flowers, amid which spring up grotesque figures of men and animals.

As to the binding, worn now, or perhaps even then, to the woof, it is in black velvet, of which the flat covers are adorned in the centre with an enamelled pansy, in a silver setting surrounded by a wreath, to which are diagonally attached from one corner of the cover to the other, two twisted silver-gilt knotted cords, finished by a tuft at the two ends.

www.ingramcontent.com/pod-product-compliance
Lightning Source LLC
Chambersburg PA
CBHW021145160426
43194CB00007B/698